D0169337

SITE GRAPHICS

NEW ENGLAND INSTITUTE OF TECHNOLOGY
LIBRARY

RICHARD L. AUSTIN, ASLA

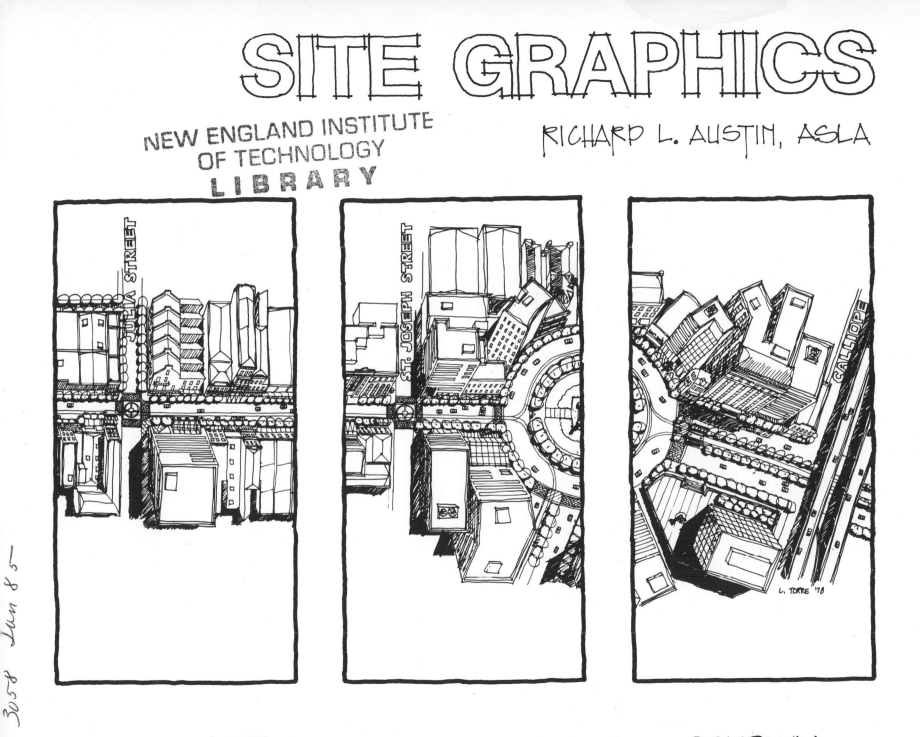

VAN NOSTRAND REINHOLD COMPANY
NEW YORK • CINCINNATI • TORONTO • LONDON • MELBOURNE

Manufactured in the United States of America
Designed by Greenplace Studios

Published by Van Nostrand Reinhold Company Inc.
135 West 50th Street
New York, New York 10020

Van Nostrand Reinhold Company Limited
Molly Millars Lane
Wokingham, Berkshire RG11 2PY, England

Van Nostrand Reinhold
480 Latrobe Street
Melbourne, Victoria 3000, Australia

Macmillan of Canada
Division of Gage Publishing Limited
164 Commander Boulevard
Agincourt, Ontario M1S 3C7, Canada

15 14 13 12 11 10 9 8 7 6 5 4 3 2 1

Library of Congress Cataloging in Publication
_____

Austin, Richard L.
    Site Graphics

    Includes index.
        1. Building Sites -- Graphic methods.
    2. Architectural design -- Graphic methods. I. Title
    NA2540.5.A97   1983   720'.28'4   83-12547
    ISBN 0-442-21077-9
    ISBN 0-442-21078-7 (pbk.)
_____

CONTENTS

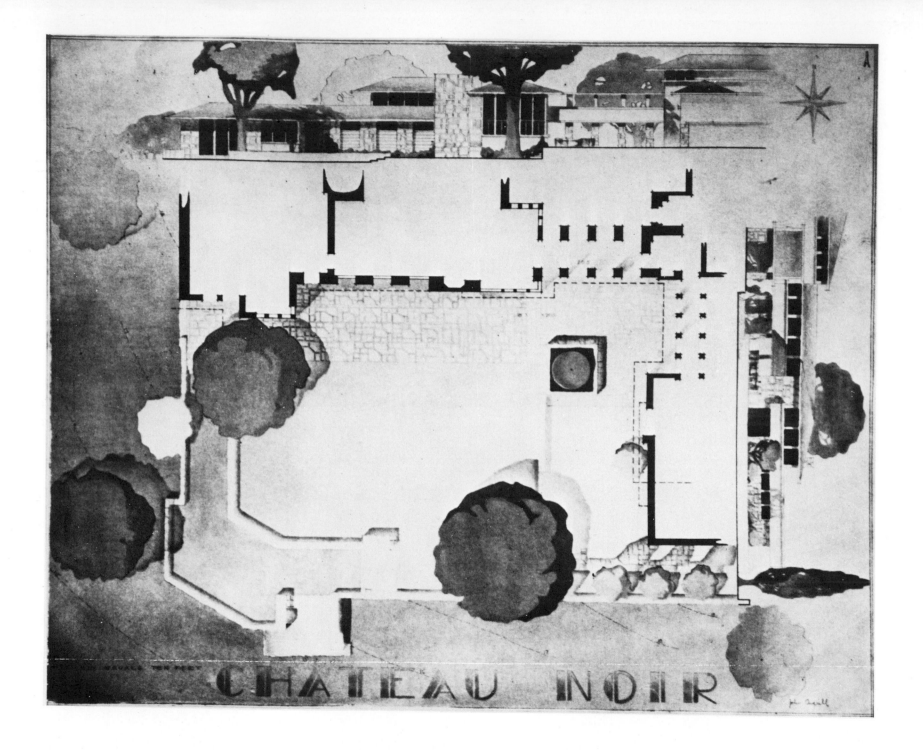

CHATEAU NOIR

FOREWORD

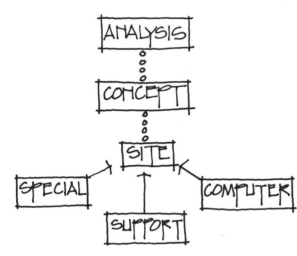

A designer should follow a basic process when developing the site graphics product. The final plan should then be reinforced by special, support, or computer graphic materials.

GRAPHICS \\'graf-iks\ n pl but sing or pl in const -the art of drawing a representation of an object on a two-dimensional surface according to mathematical rules of projection.[1]

SITE GRAPHICS \site graf-iks\ n pl but sing or pl in const - the art of drawing a representation of a site design on a two-dimensional surface (plan) according to mathematical rules of projection (scale).

GRAPHICS ARE THE DESIGNER'S PRIMARY MODE OF COMMUNICATION. WITHOUT CLEAR, CONCISE GRAPHIC TECHNIQUES, A CLIENT MAY

5

NOT UNDERSTAND THE IDEAS OR CONCEPTS OF
SITE DEVELOPMENT.

THE PURPOSE OF THIS BOOK IS TO
PROVIDE THE STUDENT OF THE ART AND THE
PROFESSIONAL IN THE FIELD WITH SAMPLE
SITE GRAPHIC TECHNIQUES. AS THERE IS A
BASIC PROCESS FOR DESIGN, THERE IS ALSO A
PROCESS FOR GRAPHIC DEVELOPMENT - AND
EACH STEP IS REPRESENTED BY AN
INDIVIDUAL CHAPTER.

USE IT AS IT IS INTENDED TO BE USED -
AS A GUIDE FOR IMPROVING THE COMMUNICATION
LINK BETWEEN YOURSELF AND THE CLIENTS
YOU SERVE.

_____

1- adapted from   WEBSTER'S NEW COLLEGIATE DICTIONARY
    G. & C. MERRIAM COMPANY, SPRINGFIELD, MASS., 1976.

THE FIRST STEP IN THE PROCESS IS ANALYSIS. CAREFUL ATTENTION SHOULD BE PAID TO THIS CATEGORY IN ORDER TO COMMUNICATE TO THE CLIENT HOW THE DESIGN DECISIONS ARE MADE.

WILDLIFE

JEFFERSON COUNTY PARK SITE

B

ARCHEOLOGICAL

JEFFERSON COUNTY PARK SITE

9

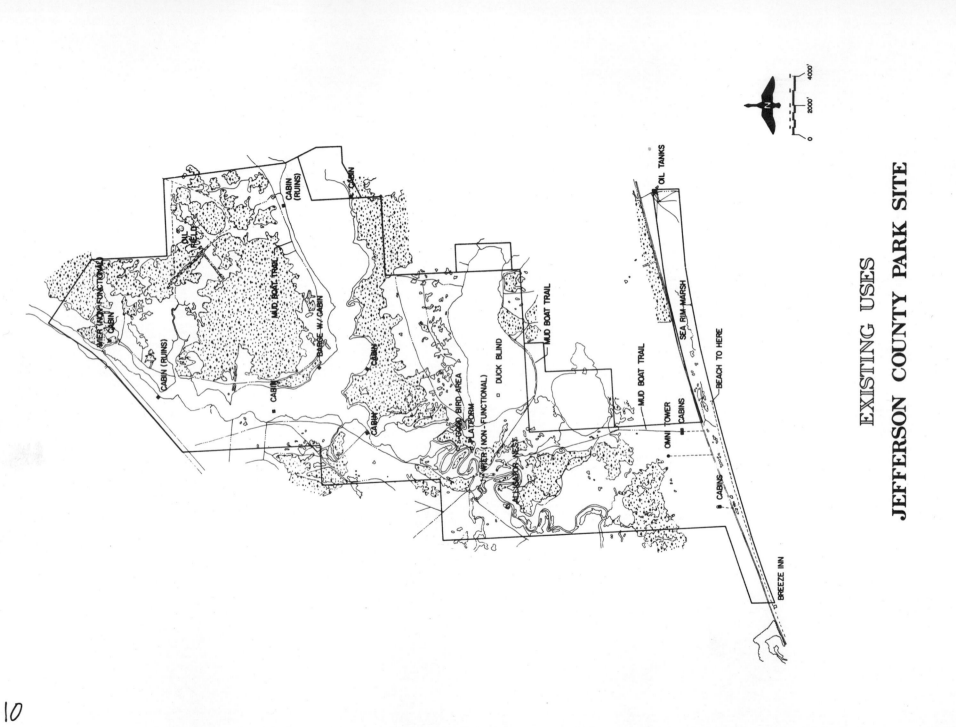

EXISTING USES
JEFFERSON COUNTY PARK SITE

10

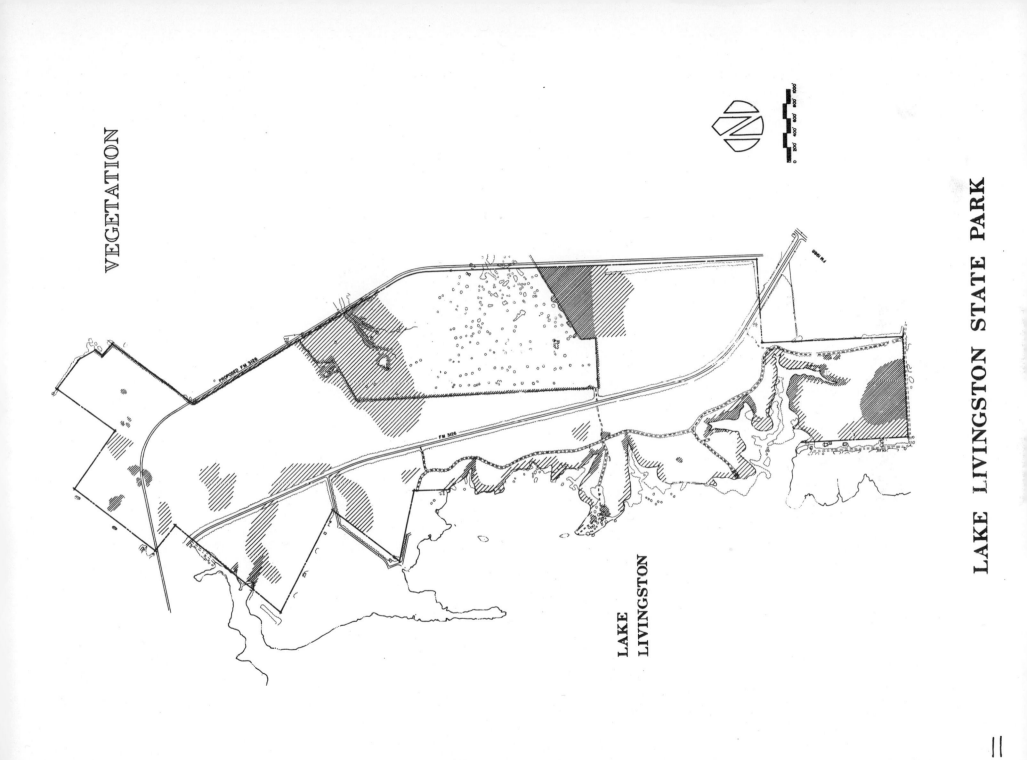

13

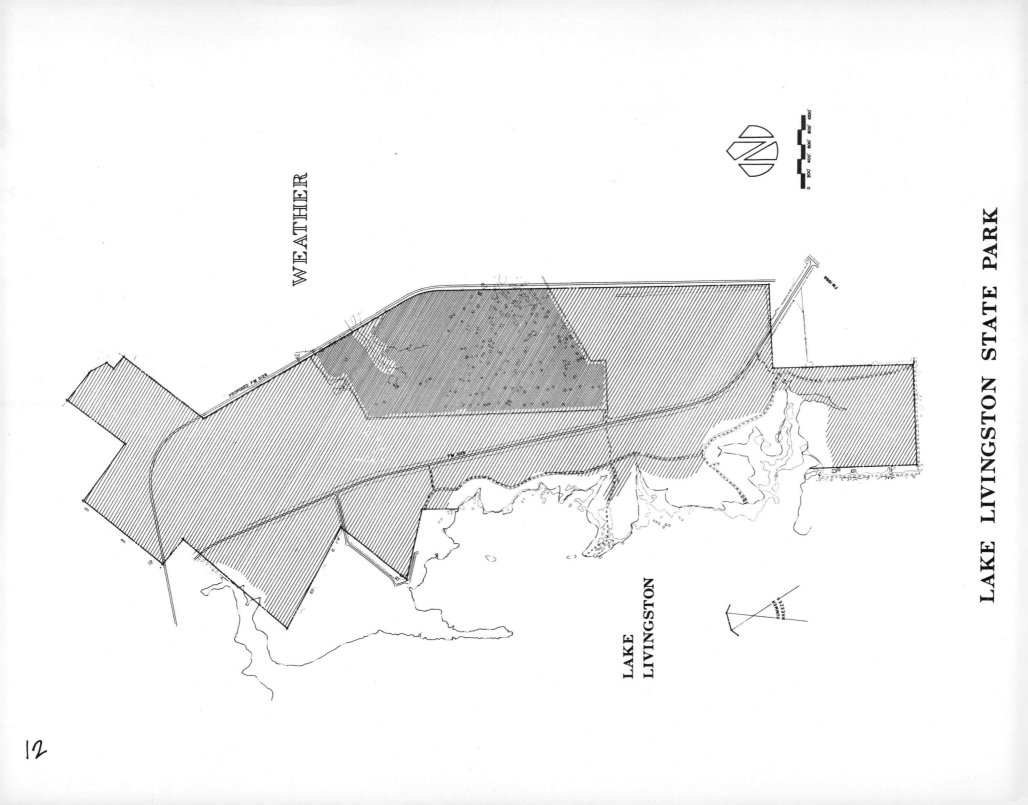

WEATHER

LAKE LIVINGSTON STATE PARK

LAKE
LIVINGSTON

12

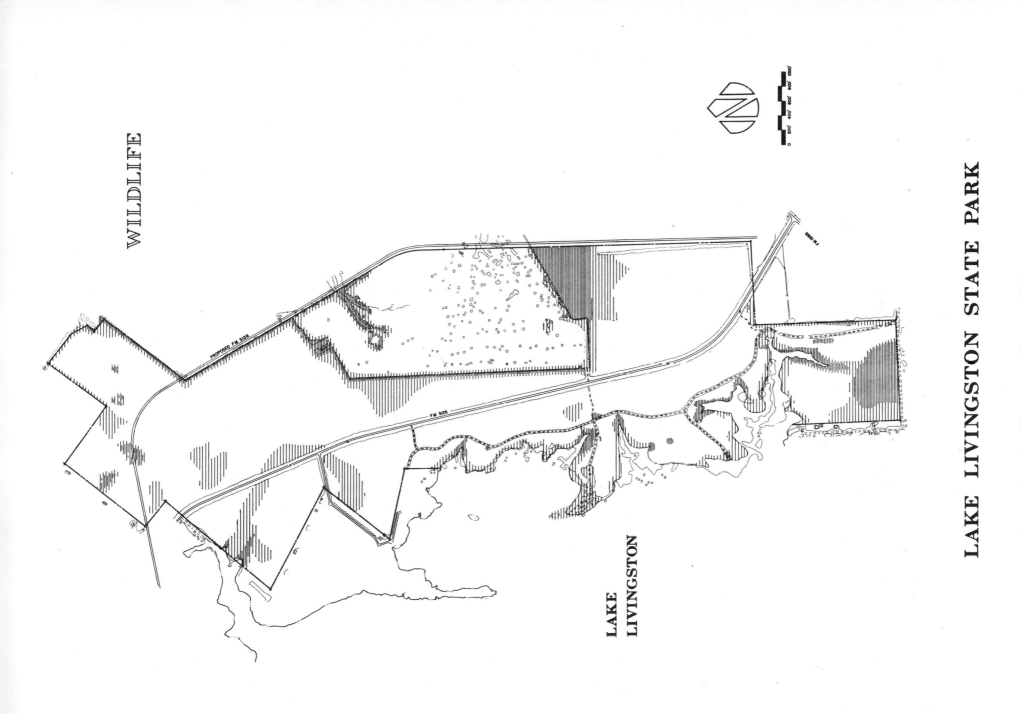

WILDLIFE

LAKE
LIVINGSTON

LAKE LIVINGSTON STATE PARK

13

VEGETATION
WILDLIFE
AESTHETICS
ARCHEOLOGICAL

VIEW

VIEW

VIEW

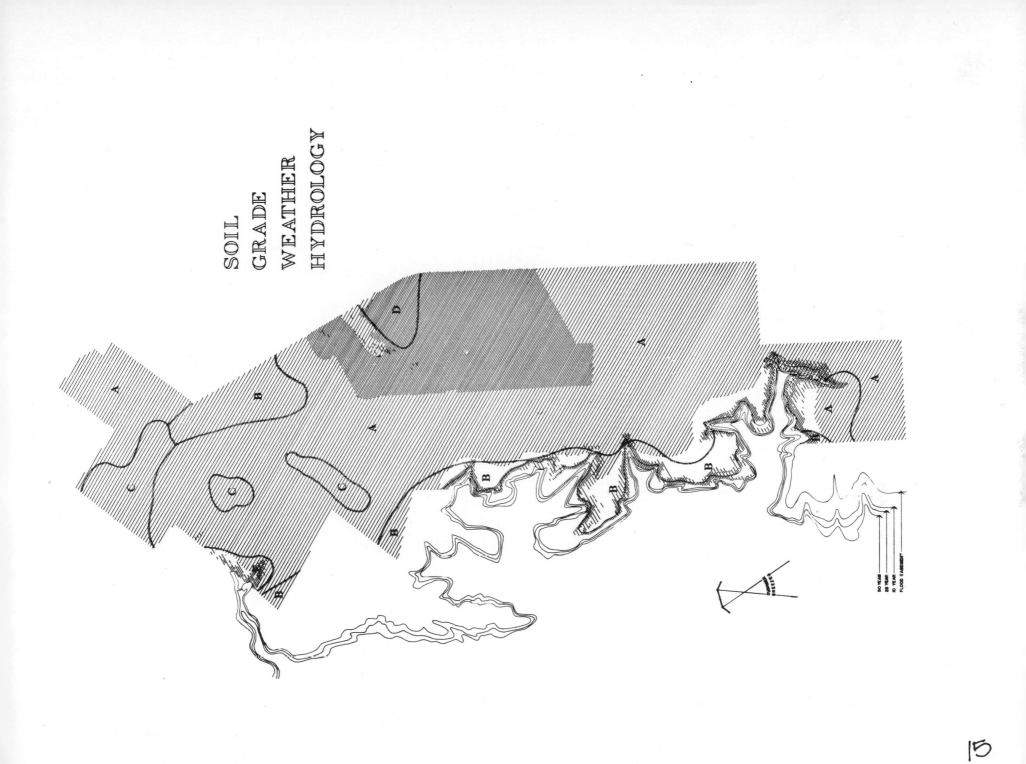

SOIL
GRADE
WEATHER
HYDROLOGY

15

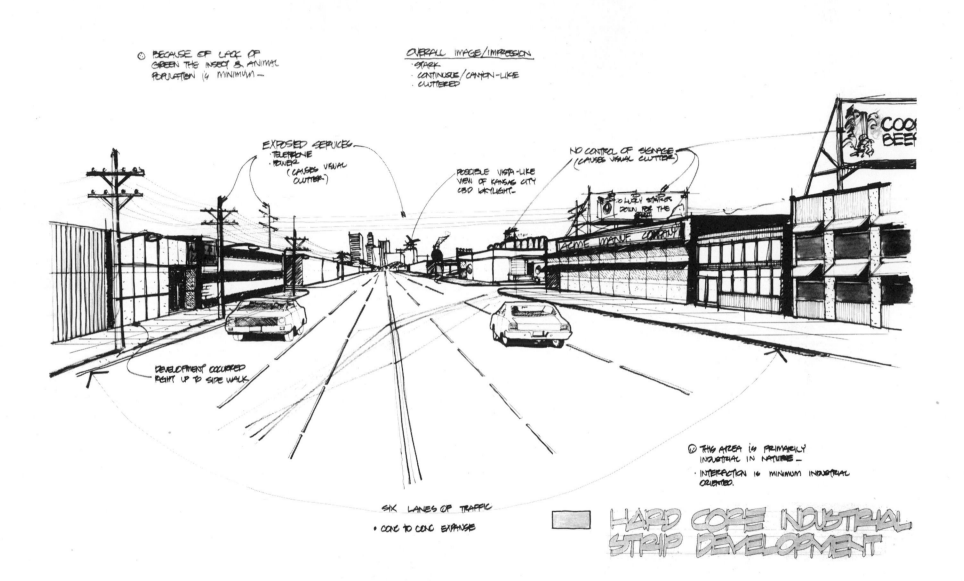

BECAUSE OF LACK OF GREEN THE INSECT & ANIMAL POPULATION IS MINIMUM —

OVERALL IMAGE/IMPRESSION
- STARK
- CONTINUOUS/CANYON-LIKE
- CLUTTERED

EXPOSED SERVICES
- TELEPHONE
- POWER
(CAUSES VISUAL CLUTTER)

POSSIBLE VISTA-LIKE VIEW OF KANSAS CITY CBD SKYLIGHT-

NO CONTROL OF SIGNAGE (CAUSES VISUAL CLUTTER)

COOK BEER

DEVELOPMENT OCCURRED RIGHT UP TO SIDE WALK

THIS AREA IS PRIMARILY INDUSTRIAL IN NATURE —
- INTERACTION IS MINIMUM INDUSTRIAL ORIENTED.

SIX LANES OF TRAFFIC
- CONC TO CONC EXPANSE

HARD CORE INDUSTRIAL STRIP DEVELOPMENT

16

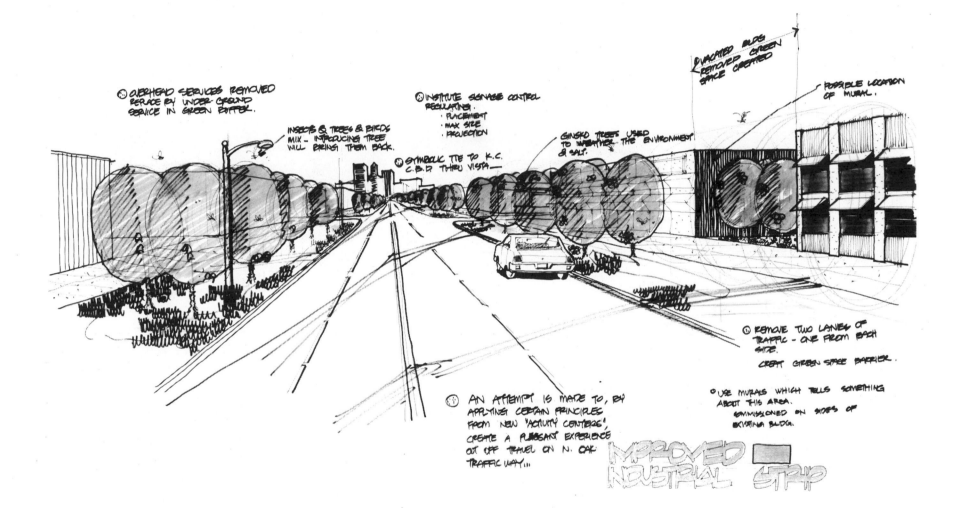

① OVERHEAD SERVICES REMOVED
REPLACE BY UNDER GROUND
SERVICE IN GREEN BUFFER.

INSECTS & TREES & BIRDS
MIX - INTRODUCING TREES
WILL BRING THEM BACK.

⑨ INSTITUTE SIGNAGE CONTROL
REGULATING:
· PLACEMENT
· MAX SIZE
· PROJECTION

⑧ SYMBOLIC TIE TO K.C.
C.B.D. THRU VISTA —

GINSKO TREES USED
TO WEATHER THE ENVIRONMENT
& SALT.

⓪ VACATED BLDG
REMOVED GREEN
SPACE CREATED

POSSIBLE LOCATION
OF MURAL.

② REMOVE TWO LANES OF
TRAFFIC - ONE FROM EACH
SIDE.
CREATE GREEN SPACE BARRIER.

⑧ USE MURALS WHICH TELLS SOMETHING
ABOUT THIS AREA.
COMMISSIONED ON SIDES OF
EXISTING BLDG.

⑪ AN ATTEMPT IS MADE TO, BY
APPLYING CERTAIN PRINCIPLES
FROM NEW "ACTIVITY CENTERS",
CREATE A PLEASANT EXPERIENCE
OUT OFF TRAVEL ON N. OAK
TRAFFIC WAY...

IMPROVED
INDUSTRIAL STRIP

17

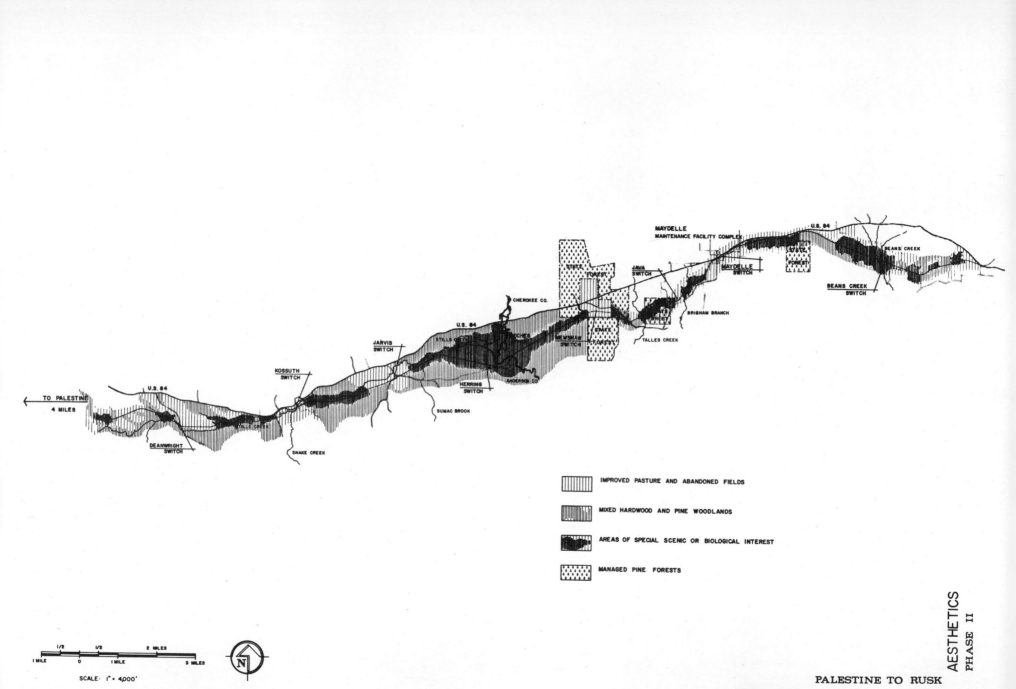

IMPROVED PASTURE AND ABANDONED FIELDS

MIXED HARDWOOD AND PINE WOODLANDS

AREAS OF SPECIAL SCENIC OR BIOLOGICAL INTEREST

MANAGED PINE FORESTS

MAYDELLE
MAINTENANCE FACILITY COMPLEX

U.S. 84

BEANS CREEK

STATE
FOREST

BEANS CREEK
SWITCH

MAYDELLE
SWITCH

JAVA
SWITCH

STATE
FOREST

BRIGHAM BRANCH

CHEROKEE CO.

STATE
FOREST

TALLES CREEK

U.S. 84

NEUGRAW
SWITCH

JARVIS
SWITCH

HERRING
SWITCH

KOSSUTH
SWITCH

U.S. 84

SUMAC BROOK

TO PALESTINE
4 MILES

SNAKE CREEK

DEANWRIGHT
SWITCH

SCALE: 1" = 4,000'

1 MILE   1/2   1/2   2 MILES
1 MILE   O   1 MILE   3 MILES

N

18

AESTHETICS
PHASE II

PALESTINE TO RUSK
STATE RAILROAD
Texas Parks and Wildlife Department

1

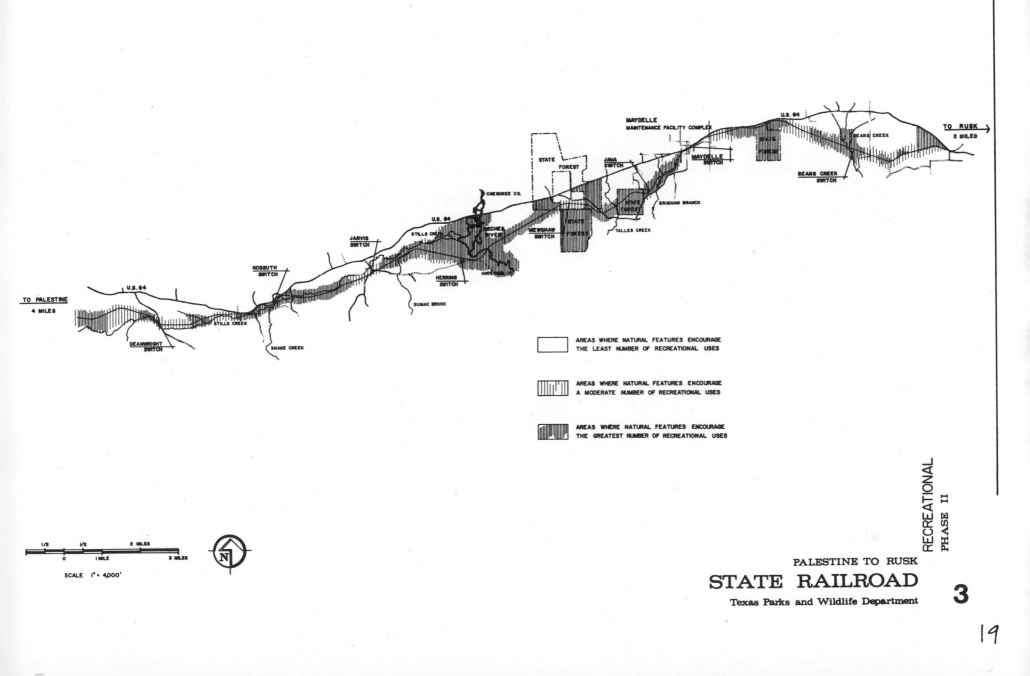

AREAS WHERE NATURAL FEATURES ENCOURAGE
THE LEAST NUMBER OF RECREATIONAL USES

AREAS WHERE NATURAL FEATURES ENCOURAGE
A MODERATE NUMBER OF RECREATIONAL USES

AREAS WHERE NATURAL FEATURES ENCOURAGE
THE GREATEST NUMBER OF RECREATIONAL USES

SCALE 1" = 4,000'

RECREATIONAL
PHASE II

PALESTINE TO RUSK
STATE RAILROAD
Texas Parks and Wildlife Department

3

19

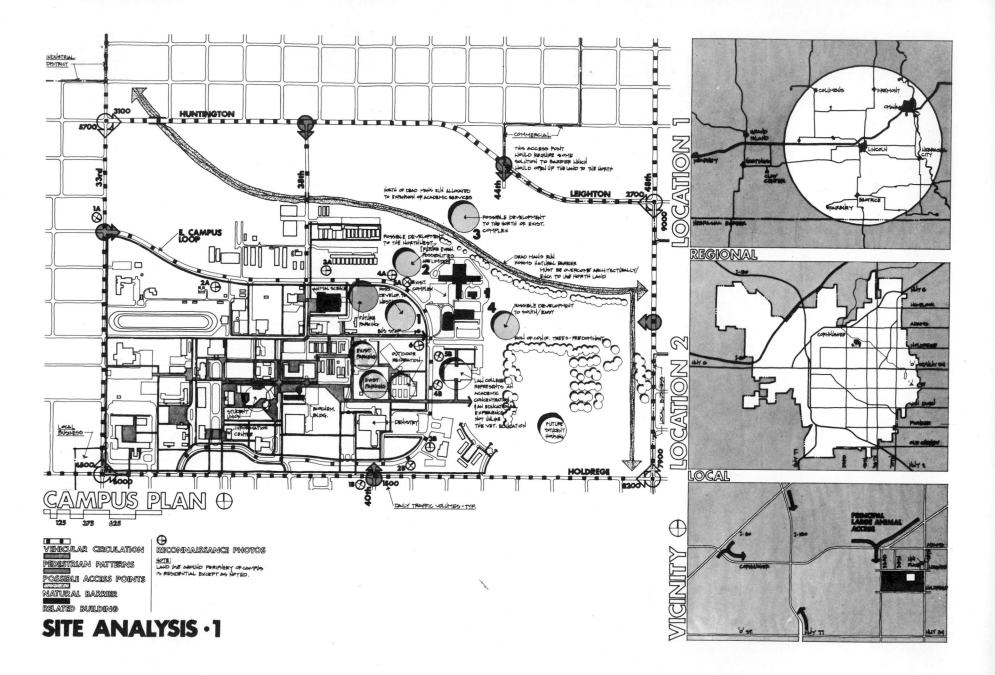

SITE ANALYSIS ·1

CAMPUS PLAN ⊕

125   175   625

VEHICULAR CIRCULATION
PEDESTRIAN PATTERNS
POSSIBLE ACCESS POINTS
NATURAL BARRIER
RELATED BUILDING

⊕ RECONNAISSANCE PHOTOS

NOTE:
LAND USE AROUND PERIPHERY OF CAMPUS IS RESIDENTIAL EXCEPT AS NOTED.

INDUSTRIAL DISTRICT

HUNTINGTON

COMMERCIAL

THIS ACCESS POINT WOULD REQUIRE SOME SOLUTION TO BARRIER WHICH WOULD OPEN UP THE LAND TO THE NORTH

NORTH OF DEAD MANS RUN ALLOCATED TO EXPANSION OF ACADEMIC SERVICES

LEIGHTON

POSSIBLE DEVELOPMENT TO THE NORTH OF EXIST. COMPLEX

POSSIBLE DEVELOPMENT TO THE NORTHWEST - (FUTURE EXPAN.) POSSIBILITIES ARE LIMITED

E. CAMPUS LOOP

DEAD MANS RUN FORMS NATURAL BARRIER MUST BE OVERCOME ARCHITECTURALLY/ ENGR. TO USE NORTH LAND

ANIMAL SCIENCE

POSS. DEVELOP. TO WEST

EXIST. COMPLEX

POSSIBLE DEVELOPMENT TO SOUTH/EAST

FUTURE PARKING

BUS STOP

ROW OF CONIF. TREES - PREDOMINANT

EXIST. PARKING

OUTDOOR RECREATION

EXIST. PARKING

LAW COLLEGE REPRESENTS AN ACADEMIC CONCENTRATION & AN EDUCATIONAL EXPERIENCE NOT UNLIKE THE VET. EDUCATION

FUTURE STUDENT HOUSING

LOCAL BUSINESS

STUDENT UNION

BIOCHEM. BLDG.

INFORMATION CENTER

DENTISTRY

HOLDREGE

DAILY TRAFFIC VOLUMES - TYP.

LOCATION 1

REGIONAL

COLUMBUS   FREMONT   OMAHA

GRAND ISLAND   LINCOLN   NEBRASKA CITY

HASTINGS

CLAY CENTER

FAIRBURY   BEATRICE

NEBRASKA BORDER

LOCATION 2

LOCAL

CORNHUSKER

SITE

VICINITY ⊕

LOCAL

PRINCIPAL LARGE ANIMAL ACCESS

CORNHUSKER

20

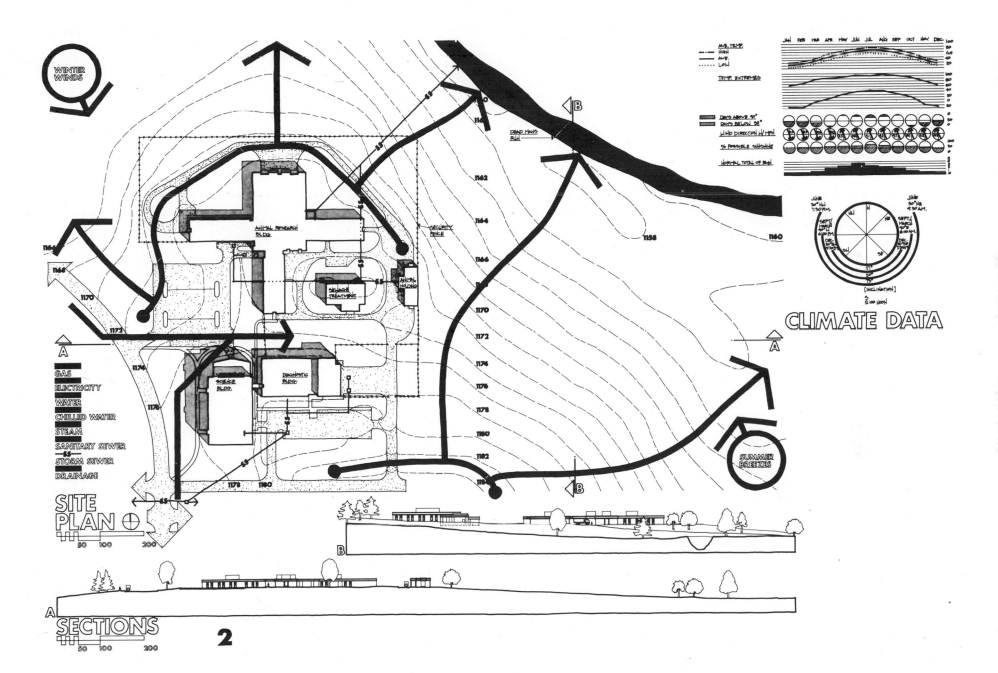

WINTER WINDS

ANIMAL RESEARCH BLDG.

SECURITY FENCE

DEAD MANS RUN

SEWAGE TREATMENT

ANIMAL HOLDING

SCIENCE BLDG.

DIAGNOSTIC BLDG.

GAS
ELECTRICITY
WATER
CHILLED WATER
STEAM
SANITARY SEWER
-SS- STORM SEWER
DRAINAGE

SITE PLAN
50   100   200

SUMMER BREEZES

CLIMATE DATA

AVG. TEMP.
HIGH
AVG.
LOW

TEMP. EXTREMES

DAYS ABOVE 90°
DAYS BELOW 32°
WIND DIRECTION W/MPH
% POSSIBLE SUNSHINE
NORMAL TOTAL OF RUN

JAN FEB MAR APR MAY JUN JUL AUG SEP OCT NOV DEC

[INCLINATION]

SECTIONS
50 100   200

2

21

SEQUENCE OF EXPERIENCES & ACTIVITIES

• AS YOU GO OUT THE WEST ENTRY:

texture: grass
use: outdoor classes

texture: concrete
use: sitting
games [paint with graphics
— map of U.S. (?)]

CONNECTOR: SLOPE

CONNECTOR: SLOPE

texture: rock garden
[grass, ground cover,
varied tree plantings
use: wind break,
shade
educational experience

texture: brick
use: play [slope becomes base
for slide, culvert pipe/
crawl spaces]

• AS YOU GO DOWN THE STAIRS:

texture: concrete area
to grass
use: basketball
tether ball
etc.

texture: concrete
use: transition area
play

texture: grass & gravel
use: play structure area

texture: grass
use: open play area

Texture: paving block with
concrete area in
center
use: passive → seating, shade
wind break
active → grid games, sand pile

CONNECTOR: SLOPE

CONNECTOR: SLOPE

texture: tree plantings,
grass, ground cover
use: wind break, shade,
winter sliding

texture: tree plantings,
grass, ground cover
use: shade, winter sliding

• AS YOU GO DOWN THE STAIRS:

texture: grass
use: large open play area

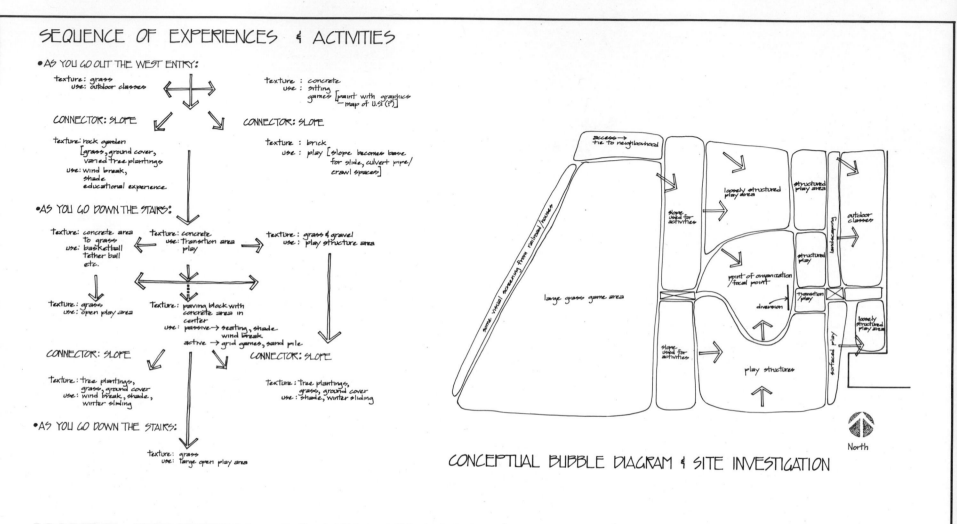

CONCEPTUAL BUBBLE DIAGRAM & SITE INVESTIGATION

North

MAUDE ROUSSEAU SCHOOL PLAYGROUND

CONCEPT: TO BETTER USE OUTDOOR SPACE, ACTIVITIES (ACTIVE/PASSIVE PLAY) ARE ORGANIZED INTO ZONES, WHICH ARE DEFINED BY
PLANTINGS AND A VARIETY OF TEXTURES.

PRELIMINARY IDEAS WILL ASSIST THE
CLIENT IN UNDERSTANDING HOW THE FINAL
PLAN WILL BE COMPLETED. THE CONCEPT
TECHNIQUE SHOULD BE USED TO BRING THE
INITIAL IDEAS INTO FOCUS.

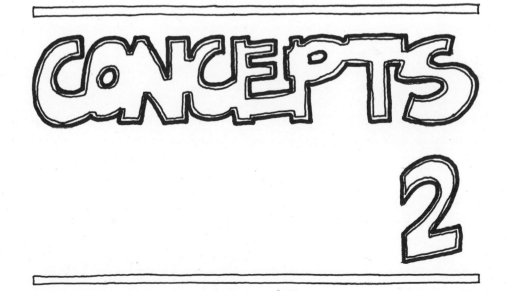

CONCEPTS

2

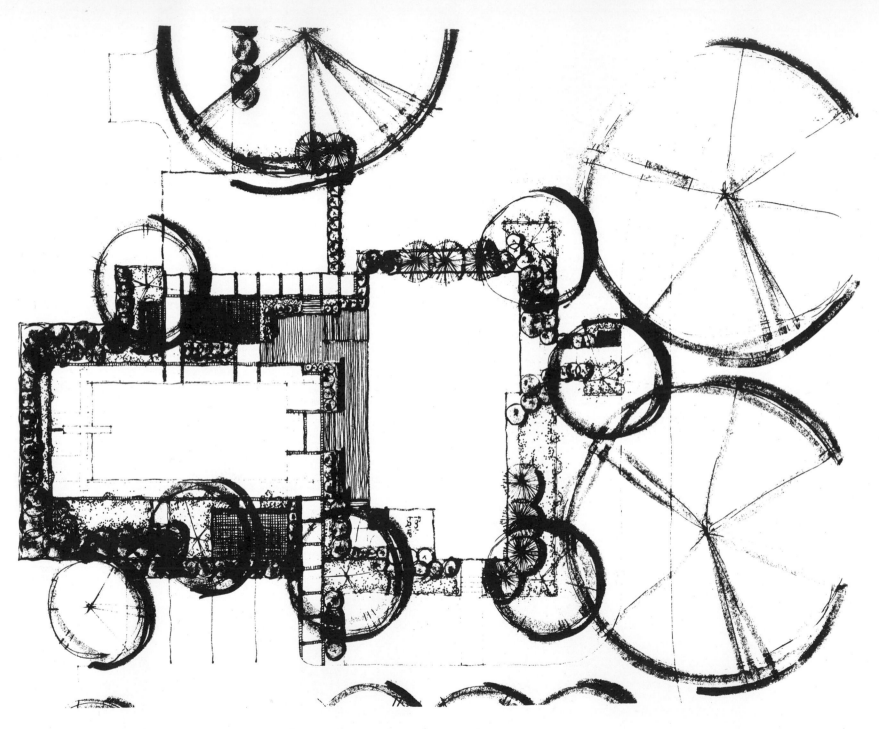

24

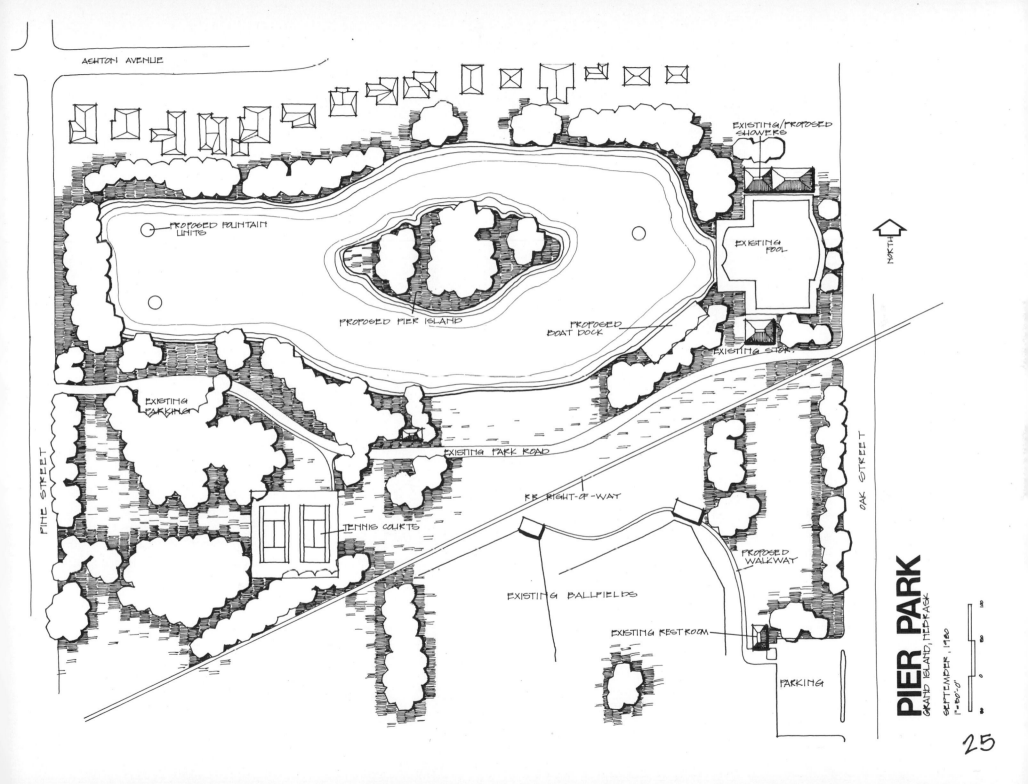

ASHTON AVENUE

EXISTING/PROPOSED
SHOWERS

PROPOSED FOUNTAIN
UNITS

EXISTING
POOL

NORTH

PROPOSED PIER ISLAND

PROPOSED
BOAT DOCK

EXISTING STOR.

EXISTING
PARKING

PINE STREET

EXISTING PARK ROAD

OAK STREET

RR RIGHT-OF-WAY

TENNIS COURTS

PROPOSED
WALKWAY

EXISTING BALLFIELDS

EXISTING RESTROOM

PARKING

PIER PARK

GRAND ISLAND, NEBRASK.

SEPTEMBER, 1980

1"=80'-0"

25

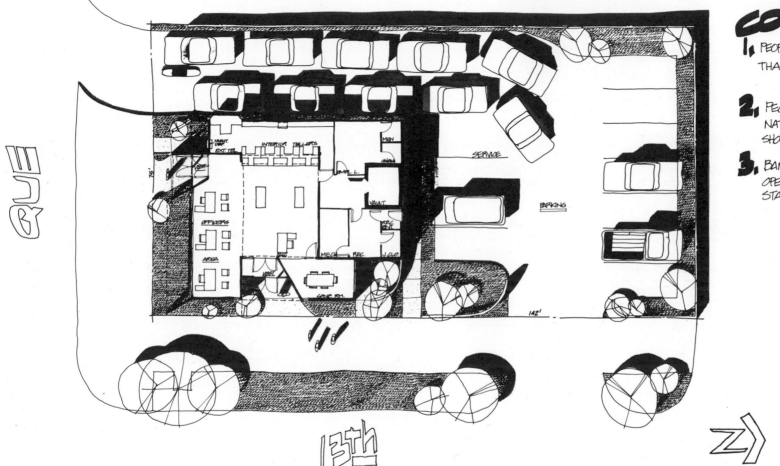

CONCEPTS

1. PEOPLE ARE MORE IMPORTANT THAN CARS.

2. PEOPLE MOVEMENT IS NATURALLY HORIZ., BANK SHOULD RELFECT IT.

3. BANK SHOULD RADIATE OPENINESS, TRUST, AND STABILITY.

26

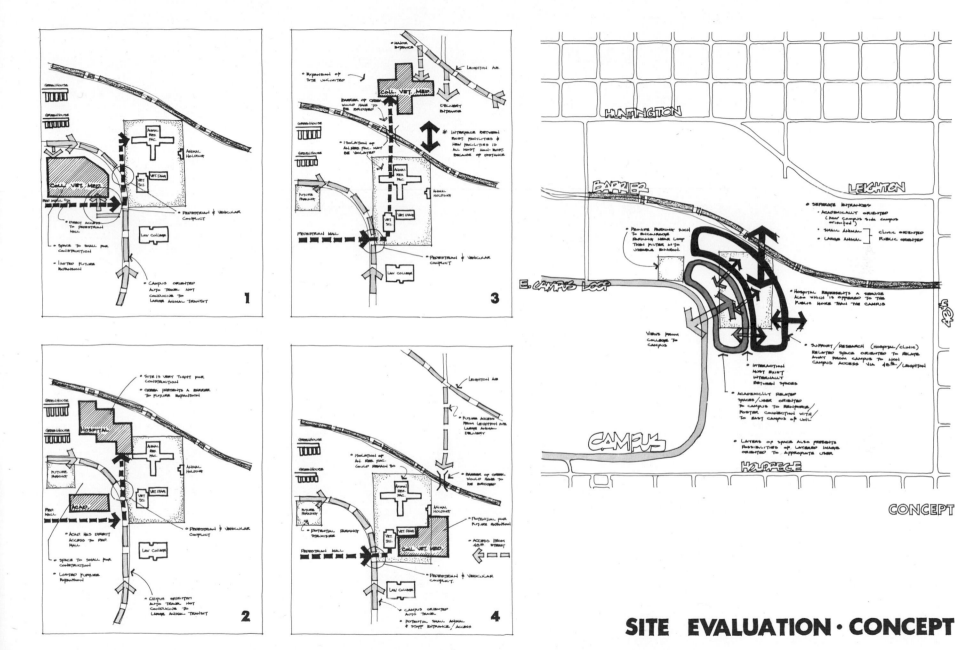

SITE EVALUATION · CONCEPT

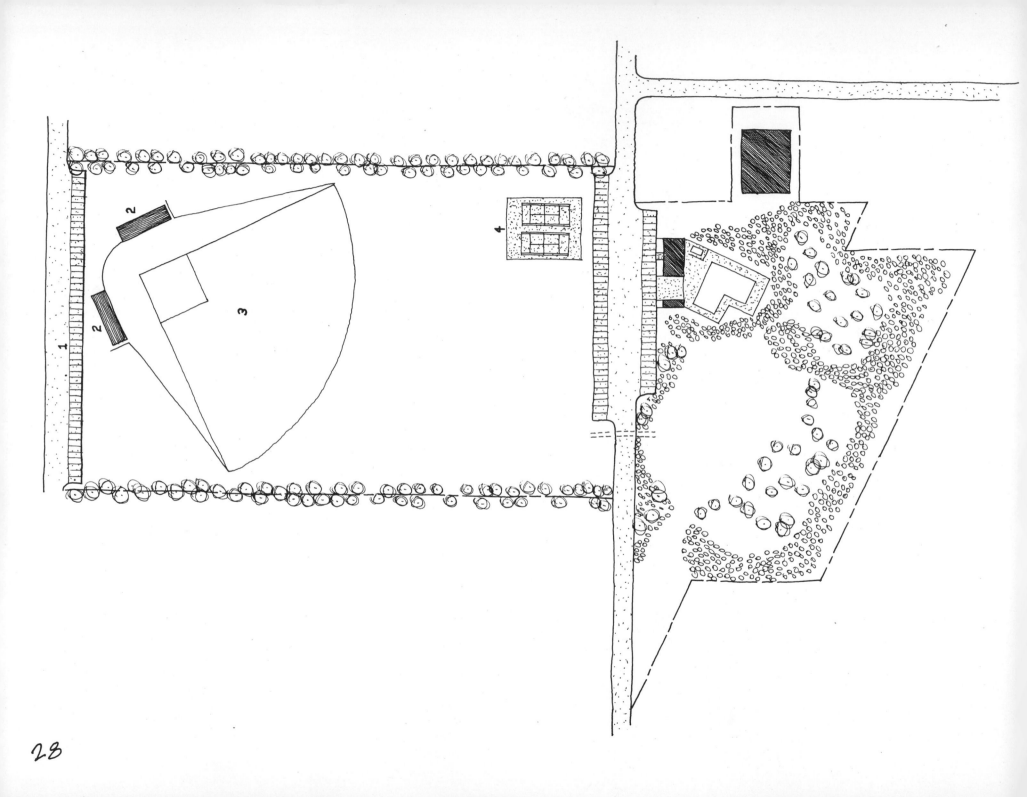

28

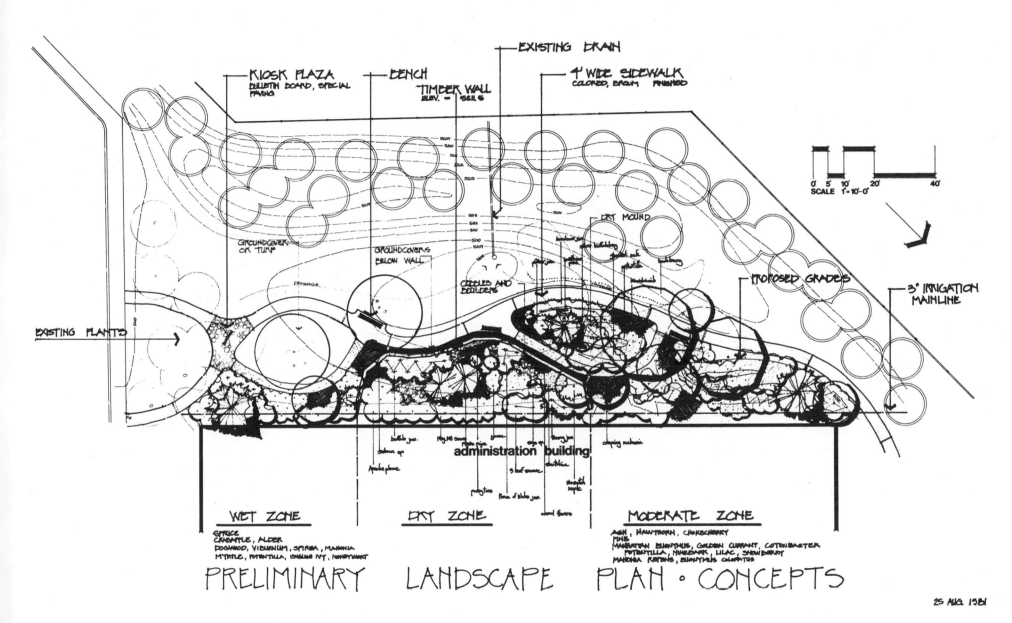

EXISTING DRAIN

KIOSK PLAZA
BULLETIN BOARD, SPECIAL PAVING

BENCH

TIMBER WALL
ELEV. — 5211.5

4' WIDE SIDEWALK
COLORED, BROOM FINISHED

DRY MOUND

GROUNDCOVER OR TURF

GROUNDCOVERS BELOW WALL

PROPOSED GRADES

3" IRRIGATION MAINLINE

EXISTING PLANTS

PEBBLES AND BOULDERS

administration building

SCALE 1'=10'-0'

0' 5' 10' 20' 40'

WET ZONE
SPRUCE
CRABAPPLE, ALDER
DOGWOOD, VIBURNUM, SPIREA, MAHONIA
MYRTLE, POTENTILLA, ENGLISH IVY, HONEYWORT

DRY ZONE

MODERATE ZONE
ASH, HAWTHORN, CHOKECHERRY
PINE
MANHATTAN EUONYMUS, GOLDEN CURRANT, COTONEASTER
POTENTILLA, NINEBARK, LILAC, SNOWBERRY
MAHONIA REPENS, EUONYMUS COLORATUS

PRELIMINARY   LANDSCAPE   PLAN · CONCEPTS

25 AUG 1981

29

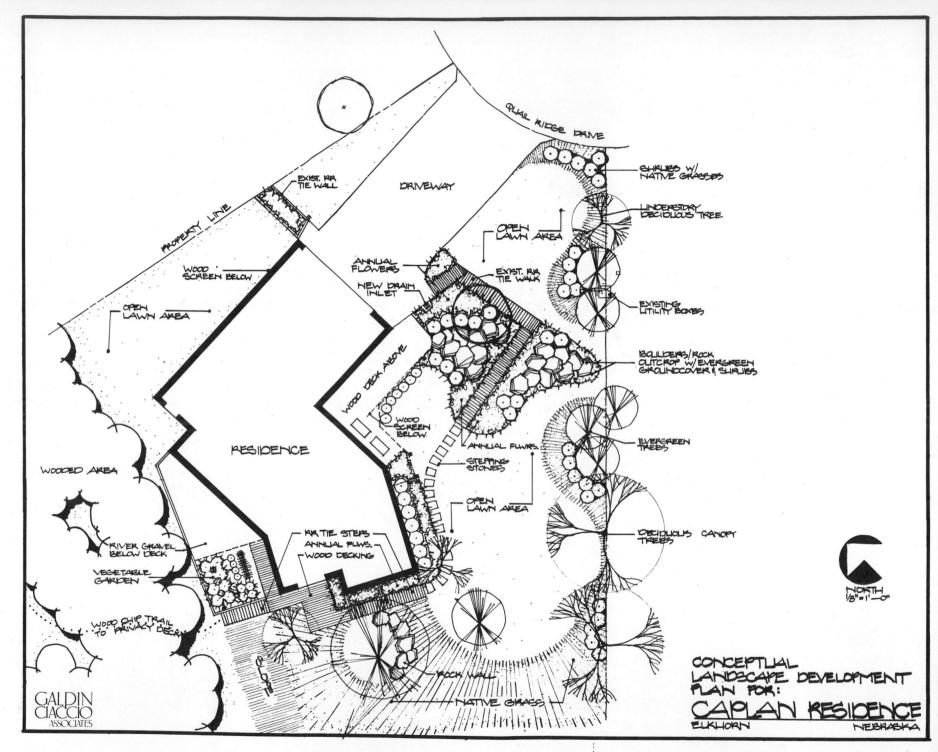

QUAIL RIDGE DRIVE

DRIVEWAY

PROPERTY LINE

EXIST. RR TIE WALL

SHRUBS W/ NATIVE GRASSES

UNDERSTORY DECIDUOUS TREE

WOOD SCREEN BELOW

OPEN LAWN AREA

ANNUAL FLOWERS

OPEN LAWN AREA

EXIST. RR TIE WALK

NEW DRAIN INLET

EXISTING UTILITY BOXES

WOOD DECK ABOVE

BOULDERS/ROCK OUTCROP W/ EVERGREEN GROUNDCOVER & SHRUBS

RESIDENCE

WOOD SCREEN BELOW

ANNUAL FLWRS.

EVERGREEN TREES

WOODED AREA

STEPPING STONES

OPEN LAWN AREA

RIVER GRAVEL BELOW DECK

RR TIE STEPS
ANNUAL FLWS.
WOOD DECKING

VEGETABLE GARDEN

DECIDUOUS CANOPY TREES

WOOD CHIP TRAIL TO PRIVACY DECK

ROCK WALL

NATIVE GRASS

NORTH
1/8" = 1'-0"

GALDIN CIACCIO ASSOCIATES

CONCEPTUAL LANDSCAPE DEVELOPMENT PLAN FOR:

CAPLAN RESIDENCE

ELKHORN   NEBRASKA

30

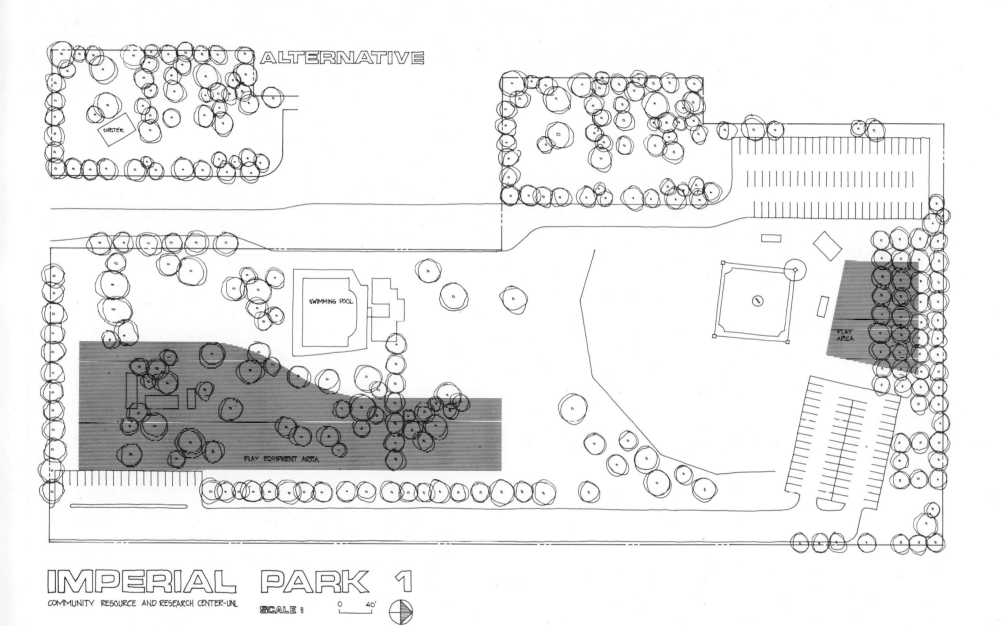

ALTERNATIVE

SHELTER

SWIMMING POOL

PLAY AREA

PLAY EQUIPMENT AREA

IMPERIAL PARK 1

COMMUNITY RESOURCE AND RESEARCH CENTER-UNL

SCALE: 0   40'

31

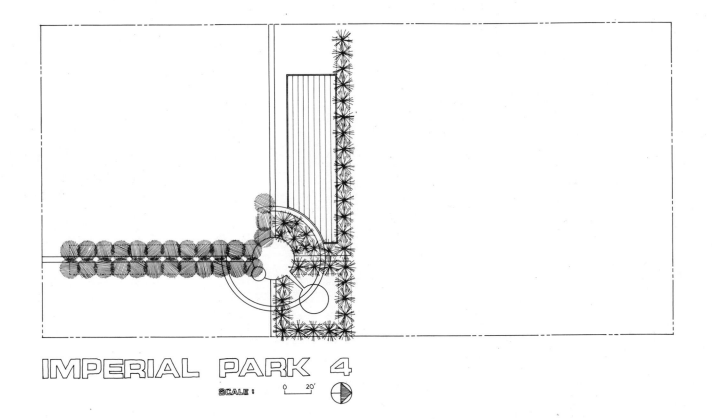

IMPERIAL PARK 4

SCALE: 0   20'

32

The site plan should represent the efforts employed to reach the final intent of the client. It is this phase of the process that will best illustrate the quality of the design program.

SITE PLANS

3

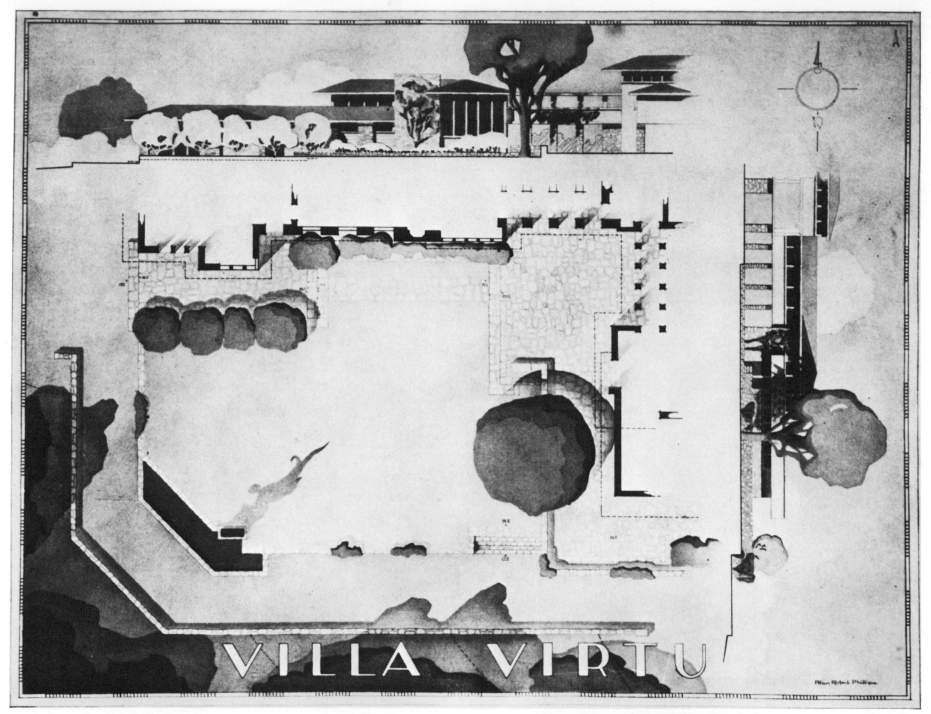

VILLA VIRTU

34

SITE DEVELOPMENT CONCEPT
GRAPHIC TECHNIQUE - CHINESE INK - 1938

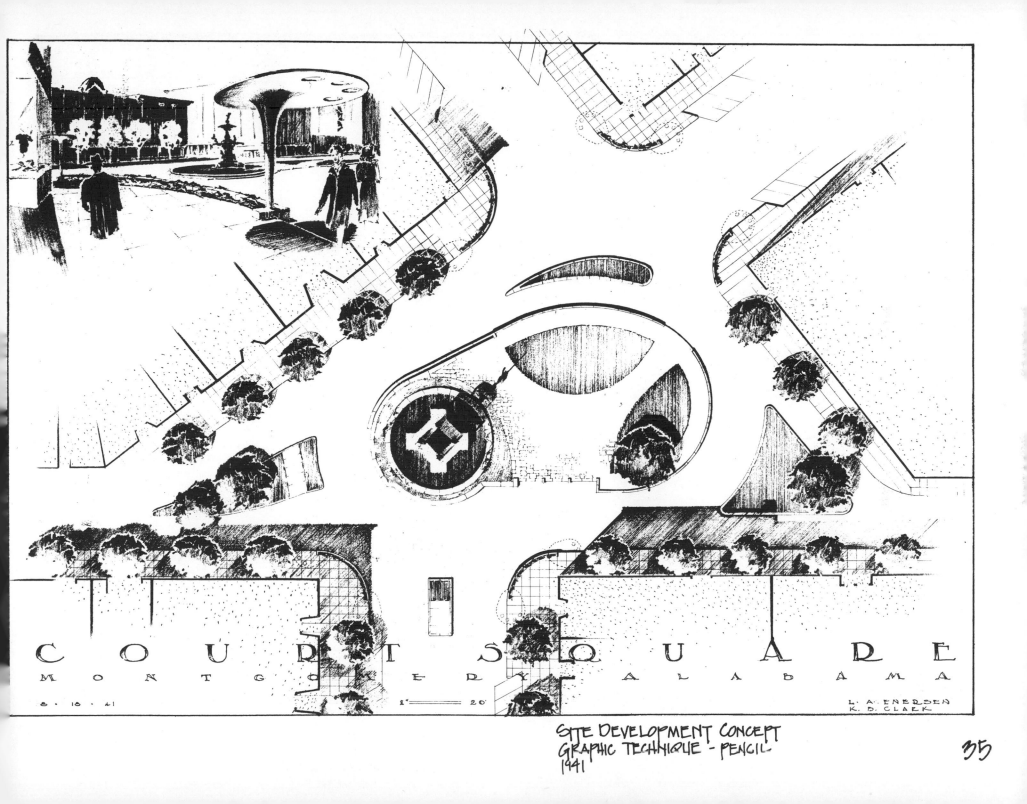

COURTSQUARE

MONTGOMERY ALABAMA

8 · 18 · 41

1" ——— 20'

L. A. ENERSEN
K. D. CLARK

SITE DEVELOPMENT CONCEPT
GRAPHIC TECHNIQUE - PENCIL
1941

35

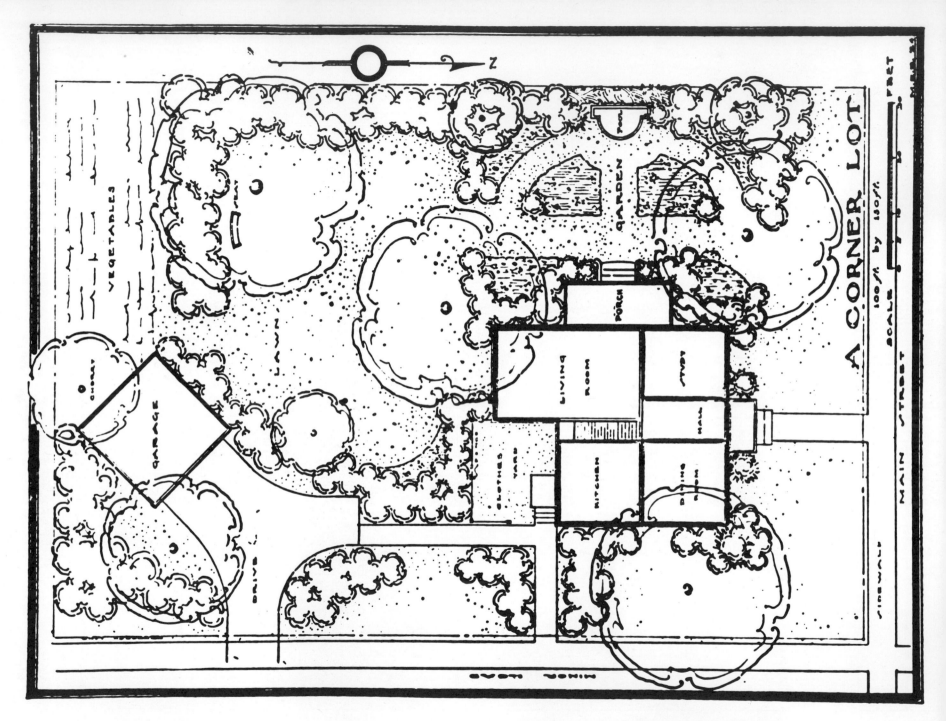

A CORNER LOT

LANDSCAPE PLANTING CONCEPT
GRAPHIC TECHNIQUE   1924

36

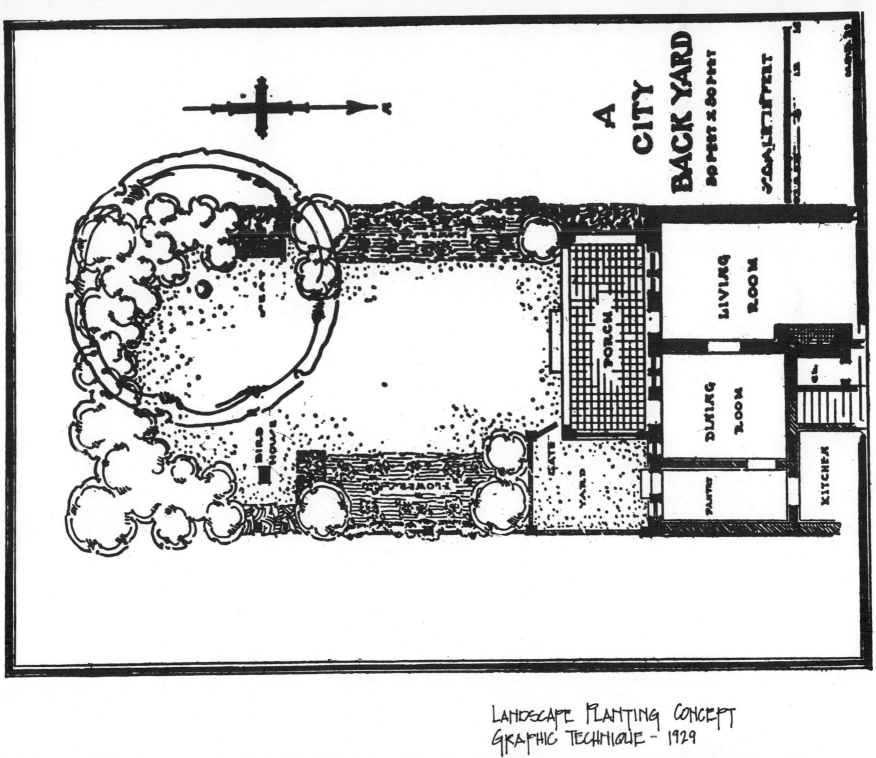

LANDSCAPE PLANTING CONCEPT
GRAPHIC TECHNIQUE - 1929

37

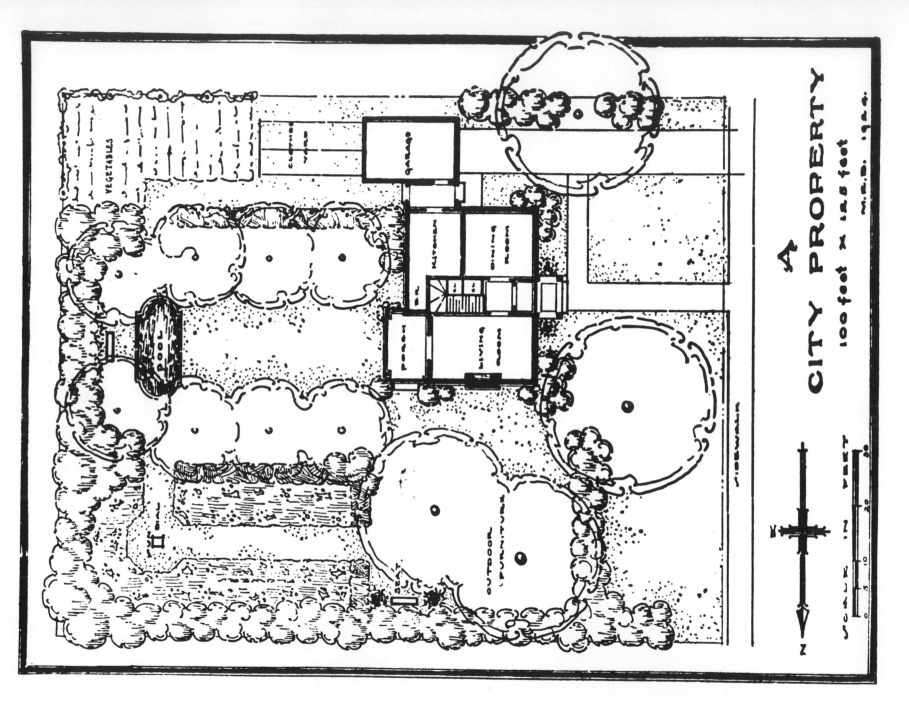

CITY PROPERTY

100 feet x 125 feet

M.E.D. 1924

LANDSCAPE PLANTING CONCEPT
GRAPHIC TECHNIQUE - 1924

38

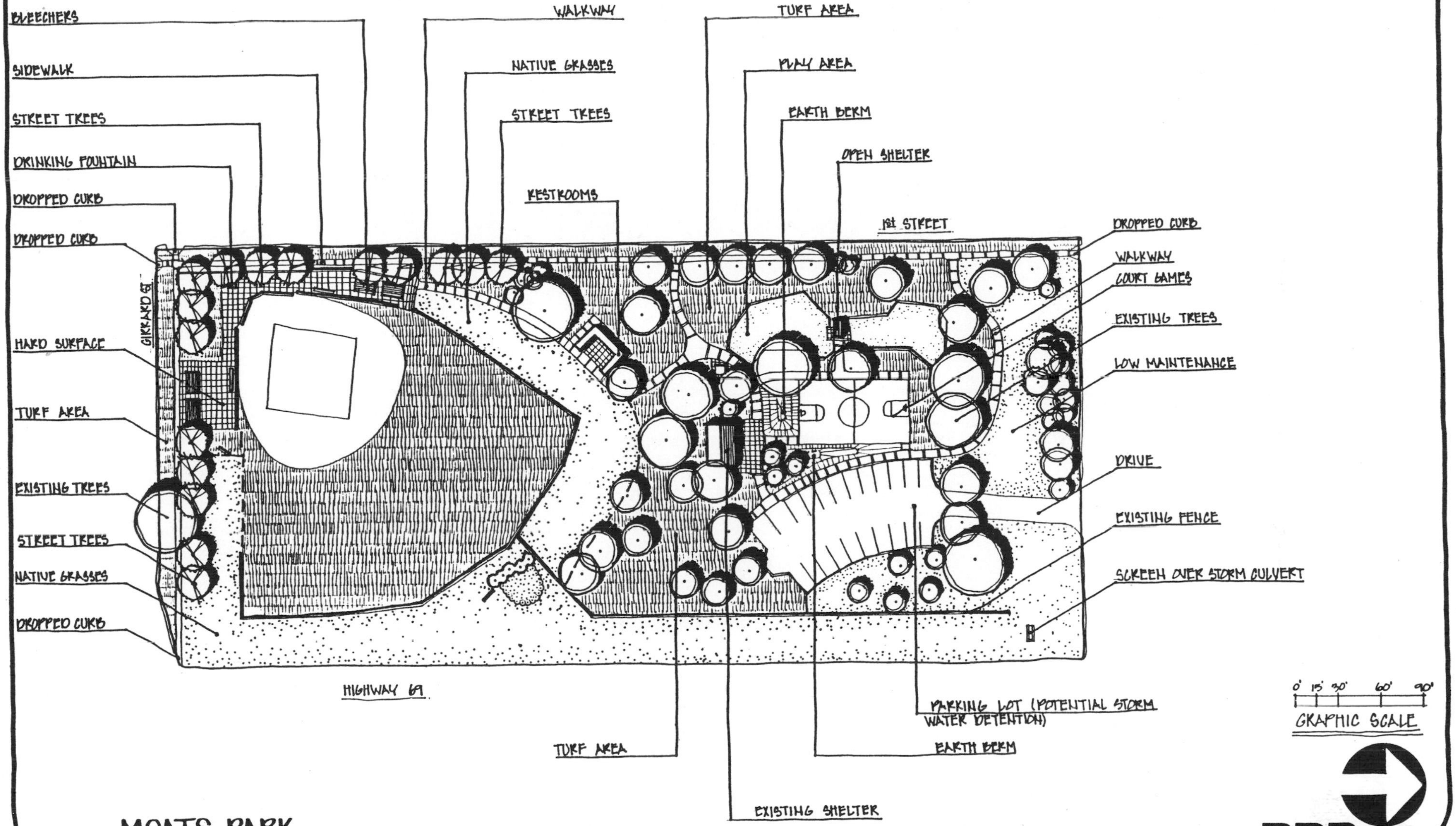

BLEECHERS

SIDEWALK

STREET TREES

DRINKING FOUNTAIN

DROPPED CURB

DROPPED CURB

HARD SURFACE

TURF AREA

EXISTING TREES

STREET TREES

NATIVE GRASSES

DROPPED CURB

WALKWAY

NATIVE GRASSES

STREET TREES

RESTROOMS

TURF AREA

PLAY AREA

EARTH BERM

OPEN SHELTER

1st STREET

DROPPED CURB

WALKWAY

COURT GAMES

EXISTING TREES

LOW MAINTENANCE

DRIVE

EXISTING FENCE

SCREEN OVER STORM CULVERT

GIRRARD ST

HIGHWAY 69

TURF AREA

EXISTING SHELTER

PARKING LOT (POTENTIAL STORM WATER DETENTION)

EARTH BERM

0' 15' 30' 60' 90'

GRAPHIC SCALE

MOATS PARK

DDP

39

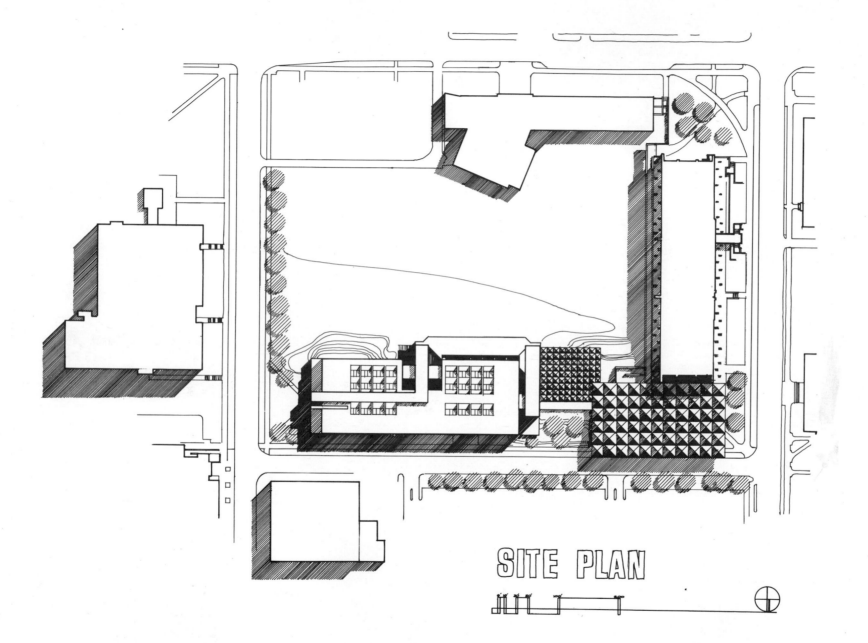

SITE PLAN

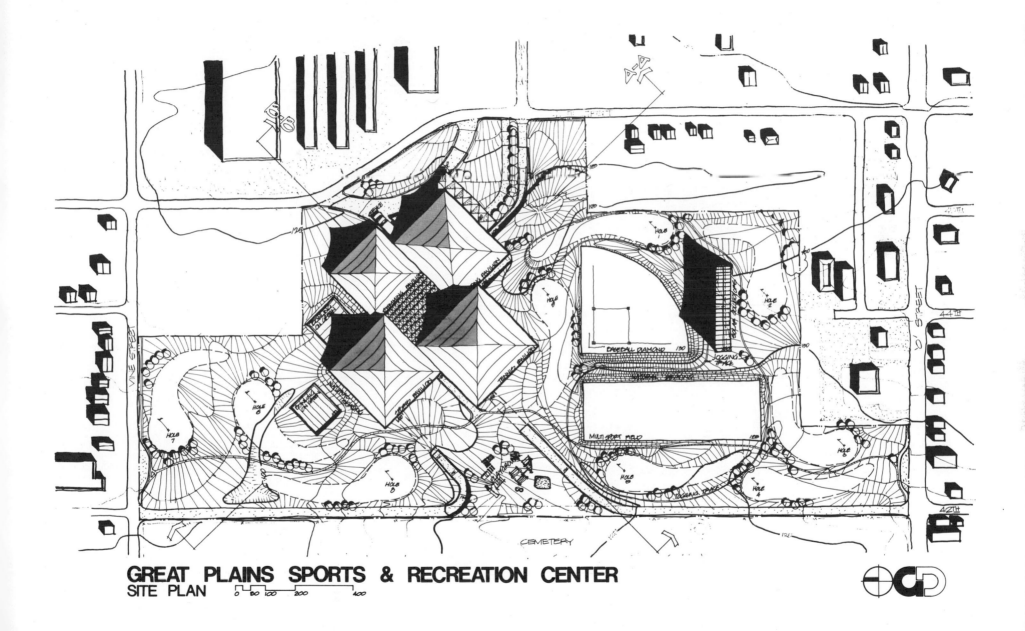

GREAT PLAINS SPORTS & RECREATION CENTER
SITE PLAN   0 50 100   200   400

41

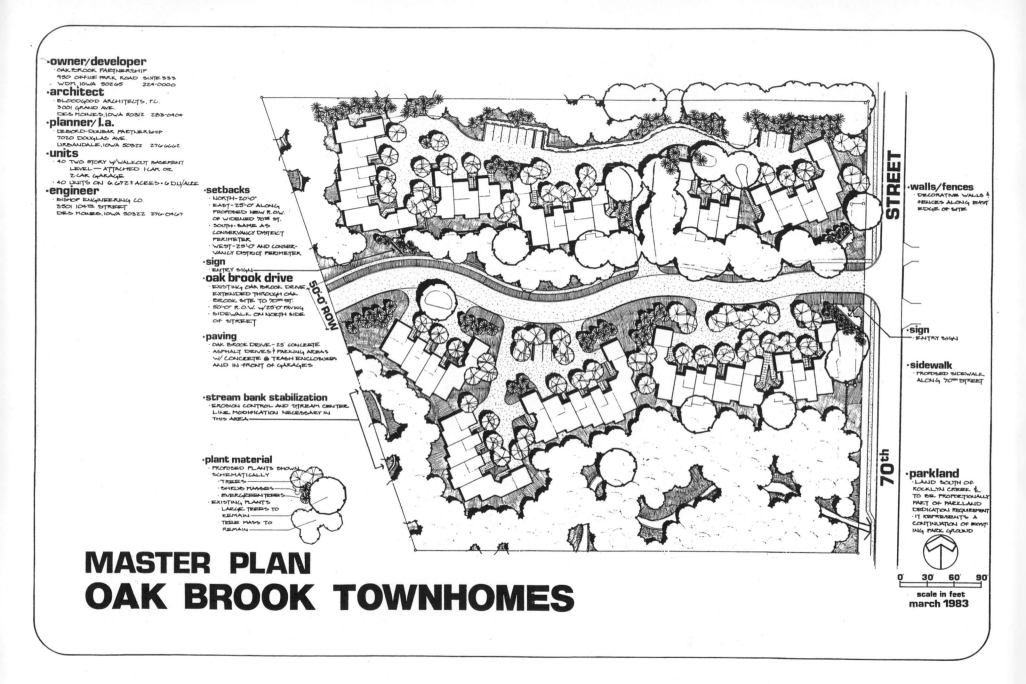

·owner/developer
OAK BROOK PARTNERSHIP
950 OFFICE PARK ROAD SUITE 333
WDM, IOWA 50265   224-0000
·architect
·BLOODGOOD ARCHITECTS, P.C.
3001 GRAND AVE.
DES MOINES, IOWA 50312 283-0404
·planner/l.a.
·DEBORD-DUNBAR PARTNERSHIP
7020 DOUGLAS AVE.
URBANDALE, IOWA 50322 276-6662
·units
· 40 TWO STORY W/WALKOUT BASEMENT
  LEVEL — ATTACHED 1 CAR OR
  2 CAR GARAGE
· 40 UNITS ON 6.672± ACRES · 6 DU/ACRE
·engineer
·BISHOP ENGINEERING CO.
3501 104TH STREET
DES MOINES, IOWA 50322 276-0467

·setbacks
· NORTH - 20'-0"
· EAST - 25'-0" ALONG
  PROPOSED NEW R.O.W.
  OF WIDENED 70TH ST.
· SOUTH - SAME AS
  CONSERVANCY DISTRICT
  PERIMETER
· WEST - 25'-0" AND CONSER-
  VANCY DISTRICT PERIMETER
·sign
· ENTRY SIGN
·oak brook drive
· EXISTING OAK BROOK DRIVE
  EXTENDED THROUGH OAK
  BROOK SITE TO 70TH ST.
· 50'-0" R.O.W. w/25'-0" PAVING
· SIDEWALK ON NORTH SIDE
  OF STREET

·paving
· OAK BROOK DRIVE - 25' CONCRETE
· ASPHALT DRIVES & PARKING AREAS
  W/ CONCRETE @ TRASH ENCLOSURES
  AND IN FRONT OF GARAGES

·stream bank stabilization
· EROSION CONTROL AND STREAM CENTER
  LINE MODIFICATION NECESSARY IN
  THIS AREA

·plant material
· PROPOSED PLANTS SHOWN
  SCHEMATICALLY
    · TREES
    · SHRUB MASSES
    · EVERGREEN TREES
· EXISTING PLANTS
    · LARGE TREES TO
      REMAIN
    · TREE MASS TO
      REMAIN

STREET

50'-0" ROW

·walls/fences
· DECORATIVE WALLS &
  FENCES ALONG EAST
  EDGE OF SITE

·sign
· ENTRY SIGN

·sidewalk
· PROPOSED SIDEWALK
  ALONG 70TH STREET

70th

·parkland
· LAND SOUTH OF
  ROCKLYN CREEK &
  TO BE PROPORTIONALLY
  PART OF PARKLAND
  DEDICATION REQUIREMENT
  IT REPRESENTS A
  CONTINUATION OF EXIST-
  ING PARK GROUND

0'   30'   60'   90'
scale in feet
march 1983

MASTER PLAN
OAK BROOK TOWNHOMES

42

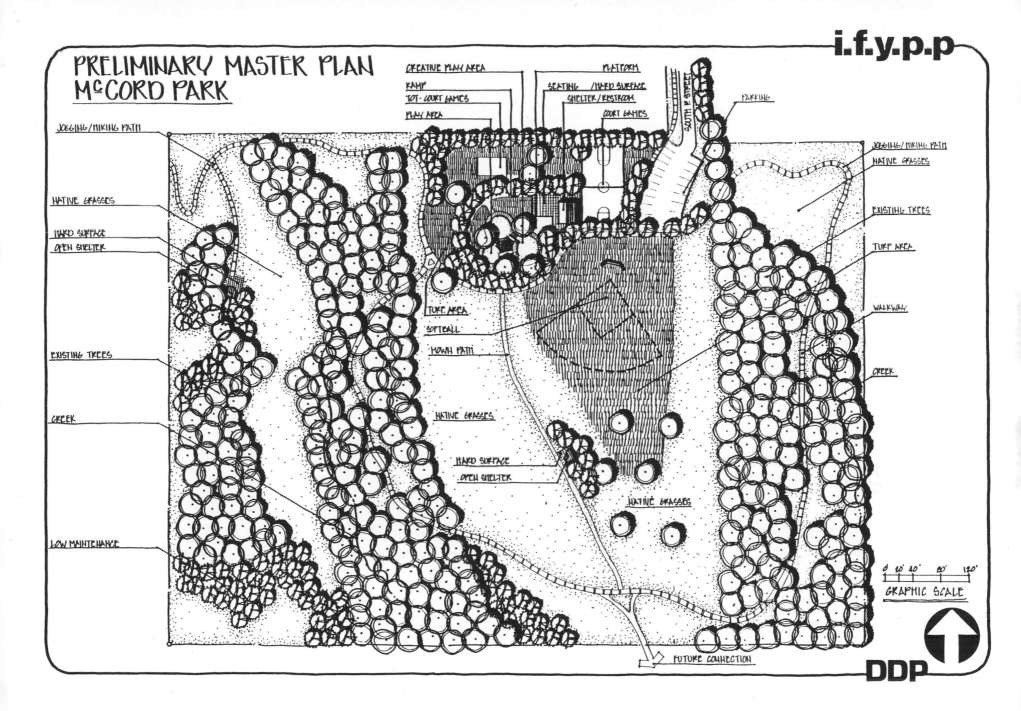

PRELIMINARY MASTER PLAN
McCORD PARK

CREATIVE PLAY AREA

PLATFORM

KAMP

SEATING /HARD SURFACE

TOT-COURT GAMES

SHELTER/RESTROOM

PLAY AREA

COURT GAMES

PARKING

JOGGING/HIKING PATH

JOGGING/HIKING PATH

NATIVE GRASSES

NATIVE GRASSES

EXISTING TREES

HARD SURFACE

OPEN SHELTER

TURF AREA

TURF AREA

WALKWAY

SOFTBALL

EXISTING TREES

MOWN PATH

CREEK

CREEK

NATIVE GRASSES

LOW MAINTENANCE

HARD SURFACE

OPEN SHELTER

NATIVE GRASSES

0 20' 40'   80'   120'

GRAPHIC SCALE

FUTURE CONNECTION

DDP

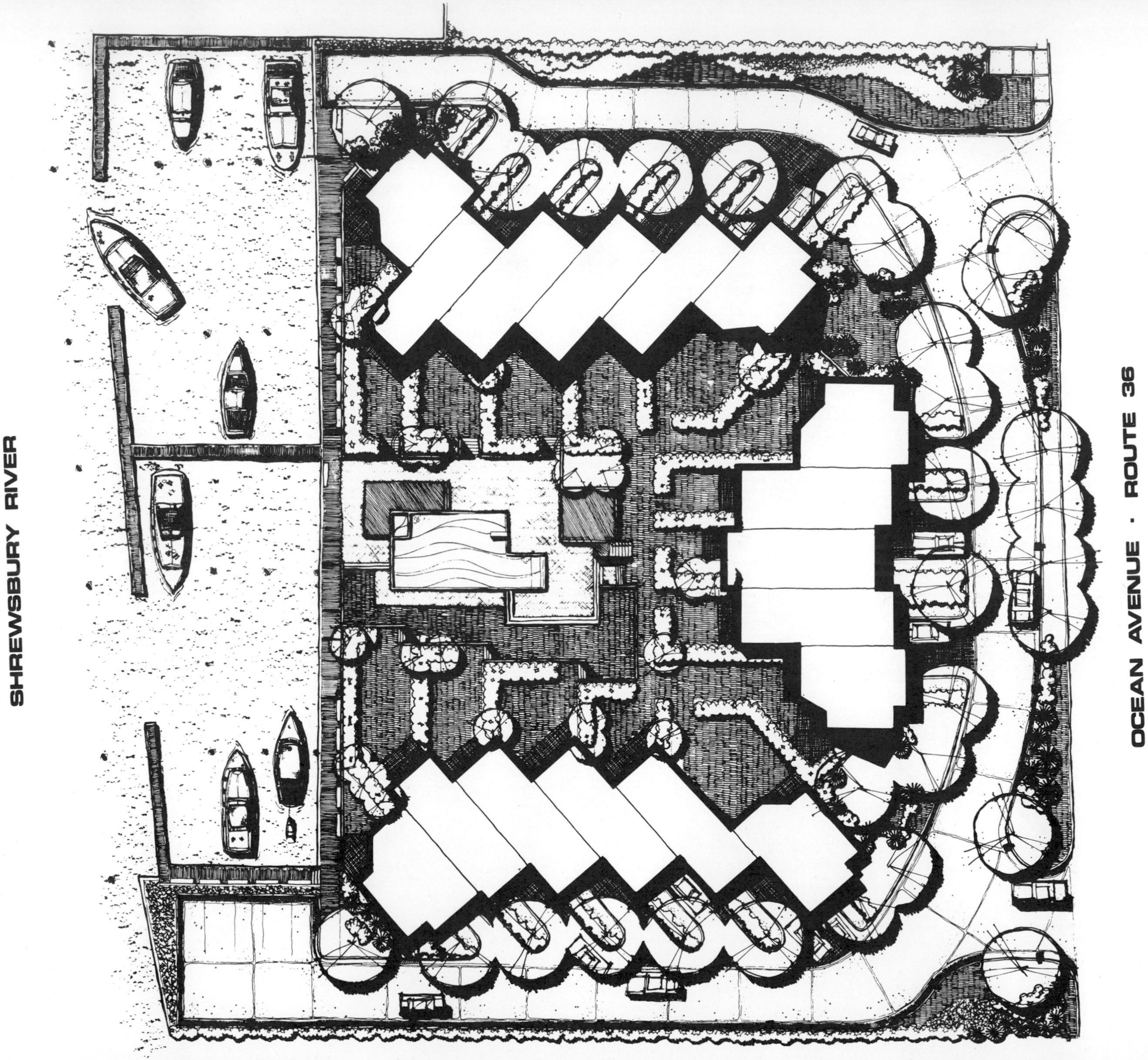

SHREWSBURY RIVER

OCEAN AVENUE · ROUTE 36

44

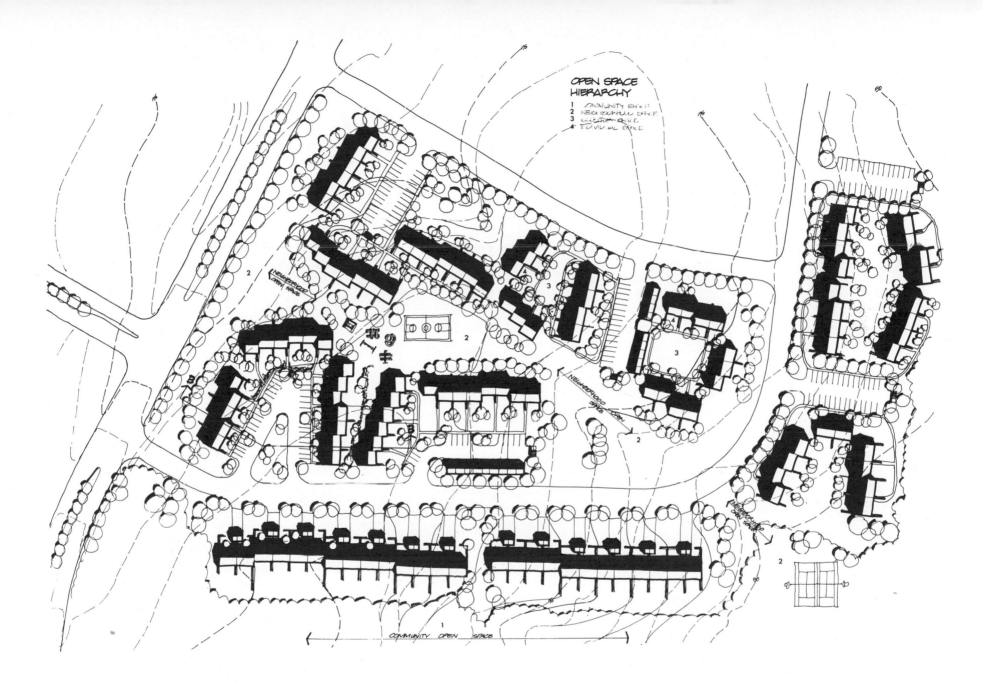

OPEN SPACE
HIERARCHY
1 COMMUNITY SPACE
2 NEIGHBOURHOOD SPACE
3 CLUSTER SPACE
4 INDIVIDUAL SPACE

NEIGHBOURHOOD OPEN SPACE

COMMUNITY OPEN SPACE

MED/HIGH DENSITY DEVELOPMENT

3.

0 25 50   100   200

45

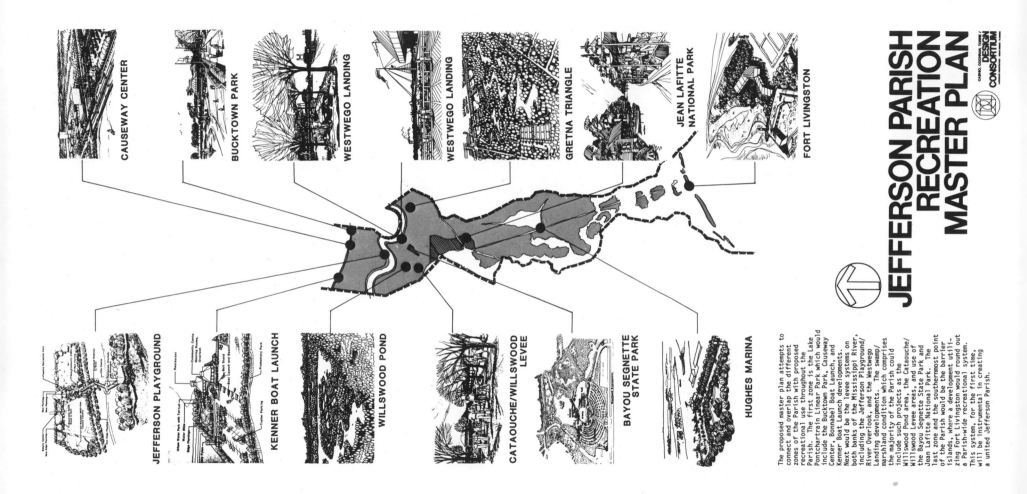

CAUSEWAY CENTER

BUCKTOWN PARK

WESTWEGO LANDING

WESTWEGO LANDING

GRETNA TRIANGLE

JEAN LAFITTE NATIONAL PARK

FORT LIVINGSTON

JEFFERSON PLAYGROUND

KENNER BOAT LAUNCH

WILLSWOOD POND

CATAOUCHE/WILLSWOOD LEVEE

BAYOU SEGNETTE STATE PARK

HUGHES MARINA

JEFFERSON PARISH RECREATION MASTER PLAN

GABRIEL, COCHRAN, TORRE DESIGN CONSORTIUM

The proposed master plan attempts to connect and overlap the different zones of the Parish with proposed recreational use throughout the Parish. The first zone is the Lake Pontchartrain Linear Park which would include the Bucktown Park, Causeway Center, Bonnabel Boat Launch, and Kenner Boat Launch developments. Next would be the levee systems on both banks of the Mississippi River, including the Jefferson Playground/ River Overlook, and the Westwego Landing developments. The swamp/ marshland condition which comprises the majority of the Parish could include such projects as the Willswood Pond area, the Cataouche/ Willswood Levee areas, and use of the Bayou Segnette State Park and Jean Lafitte National Park. The last zone and the southernmost point of the Parish would be the barrier islands, where a development utilizing Fort Livingston would round out a Parish-wide recreational system. This system, for the first time, will be instrumental in creating a united Jefferson Parish.

46

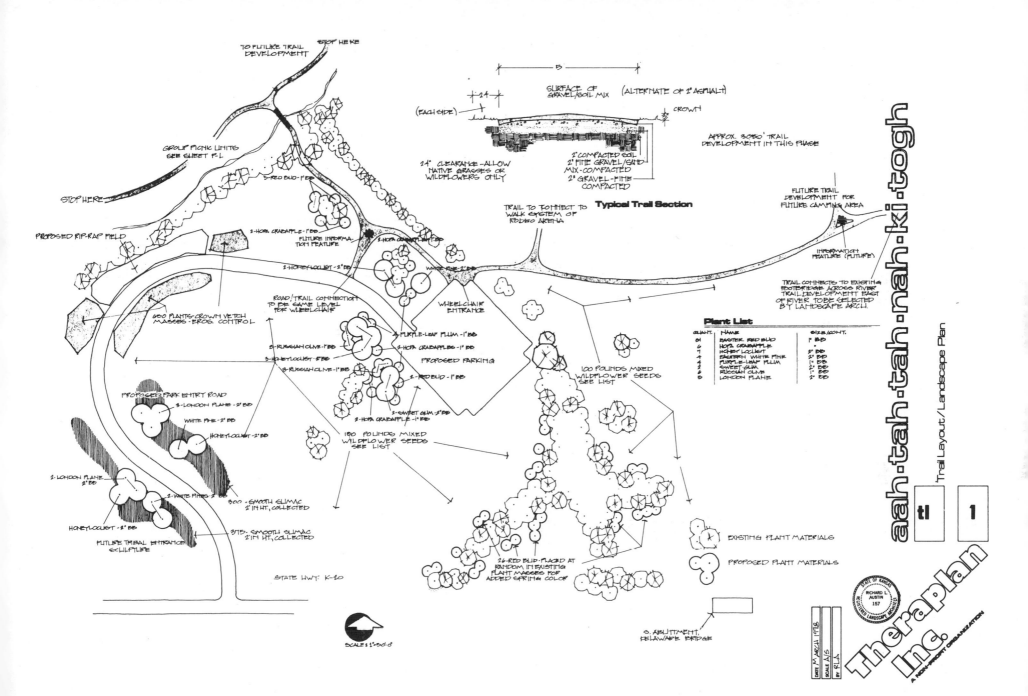

TO FUTURE TRAIL DEVELOPMENT

STOP HERE

GROUP PICNIC UNITS SEE SHEET P-L

STOP HERE

PROPOSED RIP-RAP FIELD

3-RED BUD-1"BB

2-HOPA CRABAPPLE-1"BB

FUTURE INFORMA-TION FEATURE

2-HOPA CRABAPPLE-1"BB

2-HONEY LOCUST-2"BB

WHITE PINE-2"BB

600 PLANTS-CROWN VETCH MASSES-EROS. CONTROL

ROAD/TRAIL CONNECTION TO BE SAME LEVEL FOR WHEELCHAIR

4-PURPLE-LEAF PLUM-1"BB

3-RUSSIAN OLIVE-1"BB

2-HOPA CRABAPPLES-1"BB

3-HONEYLOCUST-2"BB

PROPOSED PARKING

3-RUSSIAN OLIVE-1"BB

1-RED BUD-1"BB

PROPOSED PARK ENTRY ROAD

3-LONDON PLANE-2"BB

WHITE PINE-2"BB

HONEYLOCUST-2"BB

2-SWEET GUM-2"BB

2-HOPA CRABAPPLE-1"BB

180 POUNDS MIXED WILDFLOWER SEEDS SEE LIST

2-LONDON PLANE 2"BB

2-WHITE PINE-2"BB

300-SMOOTH SUMAC 2'IN HT, COLLECTED

HONEYLOCUST-2"BB

375-SMOOTH SUMAC 2'IN HT, COLLECTED

FUTURE TRIBAL ENTRANCE SCULPTURE

STATE HWY. K-10

WHEELCHAIR ENTRANCE

TRAIL TO CONNECT TO WALK SYSTEM OF RODEO ARENA

100 POUNDS MIXED WILDFLOWER SEEDS SEE LIST

26-RED BUD-PLACED AT RANDOM IN EXISTING PLANT MASSES FOR ADDED SPRING COLOR

S. ABUTTMENT, DELAWARE BRIDGE

SCALE: 1"=50'-0"

SURFACE OF GRAVEL/SOIL MIX (ALTERNATE OF 2" ASPHALT)

(EACH SIDE)

CROWN

APPROX. 30750' TRAIL DEVELOPMENT IN THIS PHASE

24" CLEARANCE-ALLOW NATIVE GRASSES OR WILDFLOWERS ONLY

2" COMPACTED SOIL
2" FINE GRAVEL/SAND MIX-COMPACTED
2" GRAVEL-FINE COMPACTED

Typical Trail Section

FUTURE TRAIL DEVELOPMENT FOR FUTURE CAMPING AREA

INFORMATION FEATURE (FUTURE)

TRAIL CONNECTS TO EXISTING FOOTBRIDGE ACROSS RIVER TRAIL DEVELOPMENT EAST OF RIVER TO BE SELECTED BY LANDSCAPE ARCH.

Plant List

QUANT.	NAME	SIZE/CONT.
31	EASTER RED BUD	1" BB
6	HOPA CRABAPPLE	2" BB
7	HONEY LOCUST	2" BB
4	EASTERN WHITE PINE	2" BB
4	PURPLE-LEAF PLUM	1" BB
2	SWEET GUM	2" BB
6	RUSSIAN OLIVE	1" BB
5	LONDON PLANE	2" BB

EXISTING PLANT MATERIALS

PROPOSED PLANT MATERIALS

aah·tah·tah·nah·ki·togh

Trail Layout/Landscape Plan

tl

1

STATE OF KANSAS
RICHARD L. AUSTIN
157
REGISTERED LANDSCAPE ARCHITECT

DATE: March 14, 1978
SCALE: 1/5
BY: RLA

Theraplan Inc.

A NON-PROFIT ORGANIZATION

47

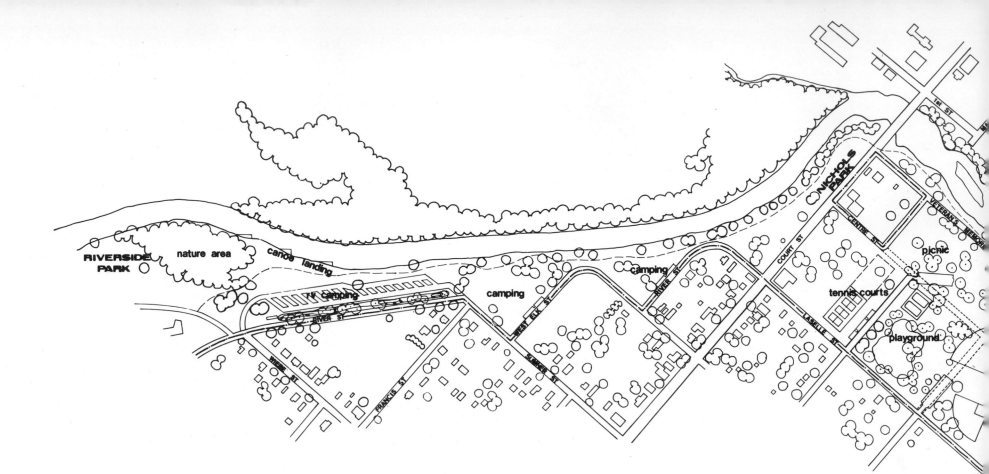

BEATRICE
RIVERSIDE PARK

PREPARED BY THE COMMUNITY RESOURCE & RESEARCH CENTER

UNIVERSITY OF NEBRASKA - LINCOLN

SCALE: 1": 200'   200 100 0   200   400

48

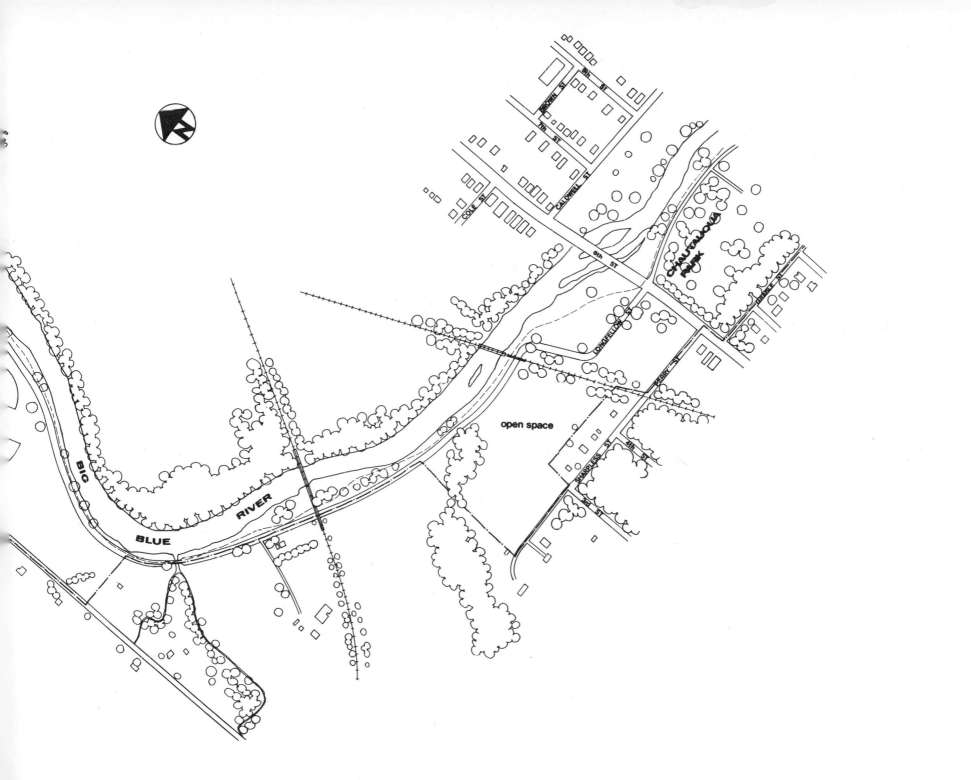

BIG
BLUE
RIVER

open space

BROWN ST
8th ST
7th ST
CALDWELL ST
COLE ST
6th ST
CHAUTAUQUA PARK
LONGFELLOW ST
PIERCE ST
SHARPLESS ST
5th ST
4th ST
3rd ST
PEARCE ST

49

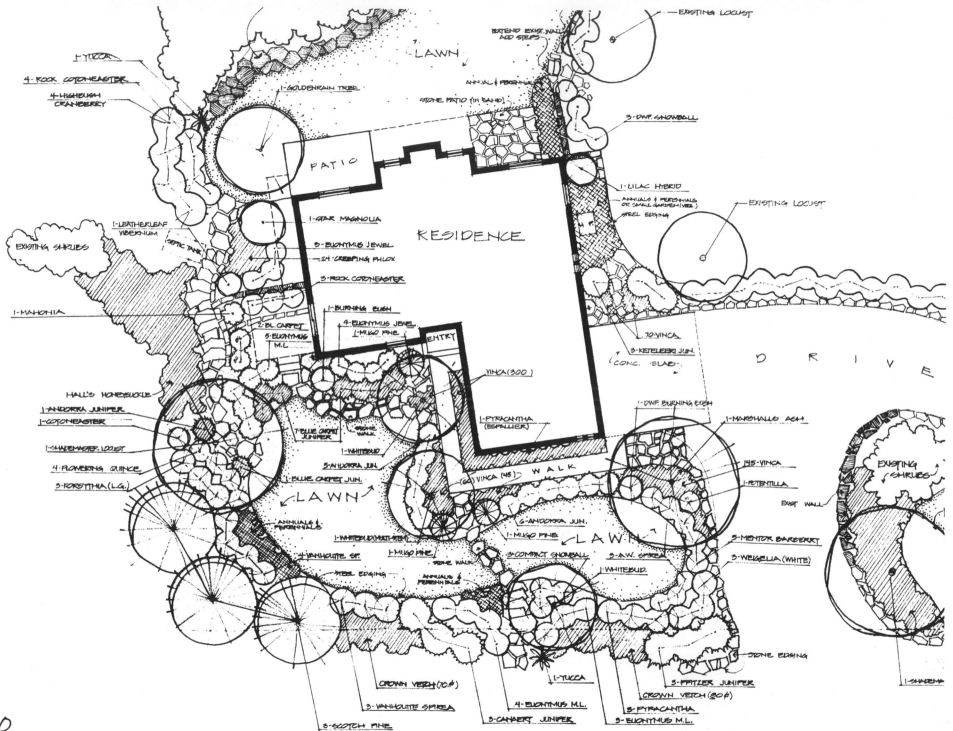

EXISTING LOCUST

EXTEND EXIST. WALL
ADD STEPS

1-YUCCA

4-ROCK COTONEASTER

4-HIGHBUSH
CRANBERRY

1-GOLDENRAIN TREE

ANNUAL & PERENNIAL

STONE PATIO (IN SAND)

3-DWF. SNOWBALL

LAWN

PATIO

1-LEATHERLEAF
VIBERNUM

EXISTING SHRUBS

SEPTIC TANK

1-STAR MAGNOLIA

1-LILAC HYBRID

RESIDENCE

ANNUALS & PERENNIALS
OR SMALL GARDEN (VEG.)

STEEL EDGING

EXISTING LOCUST

3-EUONYMUS JEWEL

24-CREEPING PHLOX

1-MAHONIA

3-ROCK COTONEASTER

1-BURNING BUSH

2-BL. CARPET

5-EUONYMUS
M.L.

4-EUONYMUS JEWEL

1-MUGO PINE

70-VINCA

3-KETELEERI JUN.

(CONC. SLAB)

D R I V E

ENTRY

VINCA (300)

HALL'S HONEYSUCKLE

1-ANDORRA JUNIPER

1-COTONEASTER

1-PYRACANTHA
(ESPALLIER)

1-DWF. BURNING BUSH

1-MARSHALLO ASH

1-SHADEMASTER LOCUST

7-BLUE CARPET
JUNIPER

STONE
WALK

145-VINCA

4-FLOWERING QUINCE

1-WHITEBUD

1-POTENTILLA

3-FORSYTHIA (L.G.)

5-ANDORRA JUN.

1-BLUE CARPET JUN.

EXIST WALL

W A L K

LAWN

(60) VINCA (45)

EXISTING
SHRUBS

ANNUALS &
PERENNIALS

6-ANDORRA JUN.

1-WHITEBUD (MULTI-STEM)

1-MUGO PINE

LAWN

5-MENTOR BARBERRY

4-VANHOUTTE SP.

1-MUGO PINE

STONE WALK

3-COMPACT SNOWBALL

3-A.W. SPIREA

3-WEIGELIA (WHITE)

STEEL EDGING

ANNUALS &
PERENNIALS

1-WHITEBUD

STONE EDGING

1-YUCCA

CROWN VETCH (70#)

5-PFITZER JUNIPER

3-VANHOUTTE SPIREA

4-EUONYMUS M.L.

CROWN VETCH (30#)

1-SHADEMA

3-SCOTCH PINE

3-CANAERT JUNIPER

3-PYRACANTHA

5-EUONYMUS M.L.

50

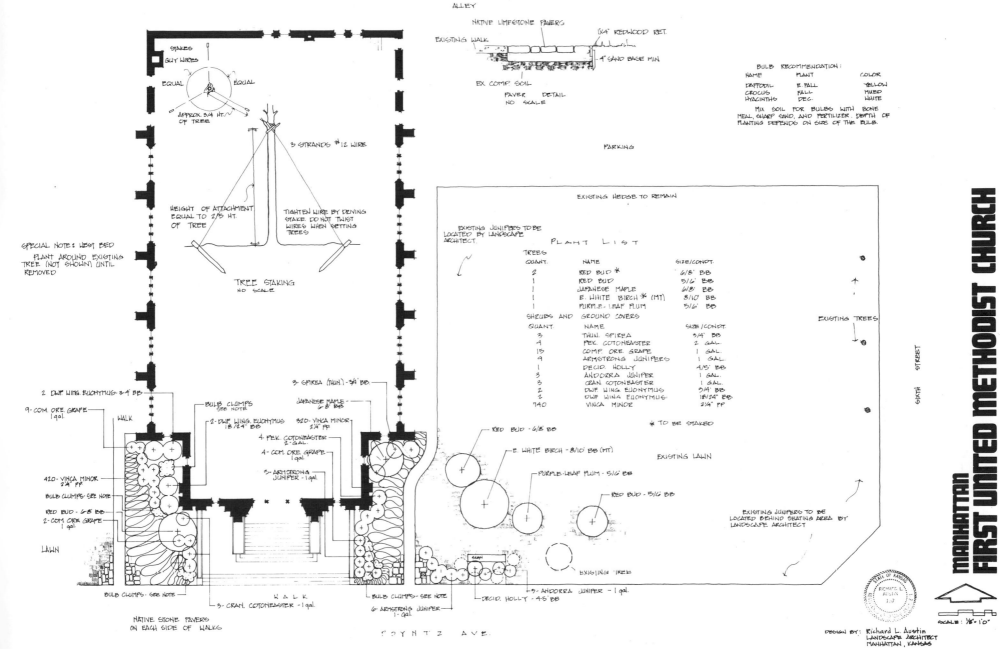

ALLEY

NATIVE LIMESTONE PAVERS

EXISTING WALK

1X4" REDWOOD RET.

4" SAND BASE MIN

EX COMP. SOIL

PAVER DETAIL
NO SCALE

PARKING

BULB RECOMMENDATION:

NAME	PLANT	COLOR
DAFFODIL	E. FALL	YELLOW
CROCUS	FALL	MIXED
HYACINTHS	DEC.	WHITE

MIX SOIL FOR BULBS WITH BONE MEAL, SHARP SAND, AND FERTILIZER. DEPTH OF PLANTING DEPENDS ON SIZE OF THE BULB.

STAKES
GUY WIRES
EQUAL   EQUAL
APPROX. 3/4 HT. OF TREE
3 STRANDS #12 WIRE

HEIGHT OF ATTACHMENT EQUAL TO 2/3 HT. OF TREE

TIGHTEN WIRE BY DRIVING STAKE. DO NOT TWIST WIRES WHEN SETTING TREES

TREE STAKING
NO SCALE

SPECIAL NOTE: WEST BED
PLANT AROUND EXISTING TREE (NOT SHOWN) UNTIL REMOVED

EXISTING HEDGE TO REMAIN

EXISTING JUNIPERS TO BE LOCATED BY LANDSCAPE ARCHITECT.

PLANT LIST

TREES

QUANT.	NAME	SIZE/CONDT.
2	RED BUD *	6/8' BB
1	RED BUD	5/6' BB
1	JAPANESE MAPLE	6/8' BB
1	E. WHITE BIRCH * (MT)	8/10' BB
1	PURPLE-LEAF PLUM	5/6' BB

SHRUBS AND GROUND COVERS

QUANT.	NAME	SIZE/CONDT.
3	THUN. SPIREA	3/4' BB
4	PEK. COTONEASTER	2 GAL.
15	COMP. ORE. GRAPE	1 GAL.
9	ARMSTRONG JUNIPERS	1 GAL.
1	DECID. HOLLY	4/5' BB
3	ANDORRA JUNIPER	1 GAL.
3	CRAN. COTONEASTER	1 GAL.
2	DWF. WING EUONYMUS	3/4' BB
2	DWF. WING EUONYMUS	18/24" BB
740	VINCA MINOR	2¼" PP

* TO BE STAKED

EXISTING TREES

SIXTH STREET

3 SPIREA (THUN.) - 3/4' BB.
JAPANESE MAPLE - 6/8' BB
320 - VINCA MINOR 2¼" PP
2 - DWF. WING EUONYMUS 18/24" BB
4 - PEK. COTONEASTER 2 GAL.
4 - COM. ORE. GRAPE 1 gal.
5 - ARMSTRONG JUNIPER - 1 gal.

2 - DWF. WING EUONYMUS - 3/4' BB
9 - COM. ORE. GRAPE 1 gal.
WALK
420 - VINCA MINOR 2¼" PP
BULB CLUMPS - SEE NOTE
RED BUD - 6/8' BB
2 - COM. ORE. GRAPE 1 gal.
LAWN
BULB CLUMPS - SEE NOTE

RED BUD - 6/8' BB

E. WHITE BIRCH - 8/10' BB (MT)

EXISTING LAWN

PURPLE-LEAF PLUM - 5/6' BB

RED BUD - 5/6' BB

EXISTING JUNIPERS TO BE LOCATED BEHIND SEATING AREA BY LANDSCAPE ARCHITECT

BULB CLUMPS SEE NOTE

EXISTING TREE

EVAN

3 - ANDORRA JUNIPER - 1 gal.

DECID. HOLLY - 4/5' BB

NATIVE STONE PAVERS ON EACH SIDE OF WALKS

BULB CLUMPS - SEE NOTE
3 - CRAN. COTONEASTER - 1 gal.
WALK
BULB CLUMPS - SEE NOTE
6 - ARMSTRONG JUNIPER - 1 gal.

POYNTZ AVE.

SCALE : ⅛" = 1'0"

DESIGN BY: Richard L. Austin
LANDSCAPE ARCHITECT
MANHATTAN, KANSAS

MANHATTAN
FIRST UNITED METHODIST CHURCH

51

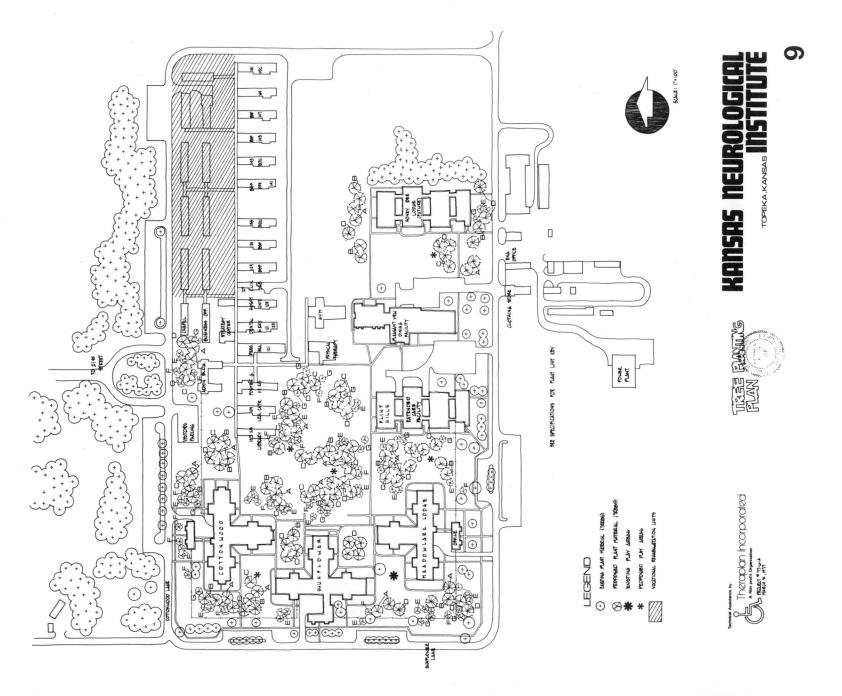

LEGEND

⊙	EXISTING PLANT MATERIAL (TREES)
⊗	PROPOSED PLANT MATERIAL (TREES)
✳	EXISTING PLAY AREAS
✱	PROPOSED PLAY AREAS
▨	VOCATIONAL REHABILITATION UNITS

SEE SPECIFICATIONS FOR PLANT LIST KEY

SCALE: 1"=100'

KANSAS NEUROLOGICAL INSTITUTE

TOPEKA, KANSAS

9

TREE PLANTING PLAN

Technical Assistance by:

Theraplan Incorporated

A Non-profit Organization

PROJECT #TP-IV-A
MARCH 14, 1977

52

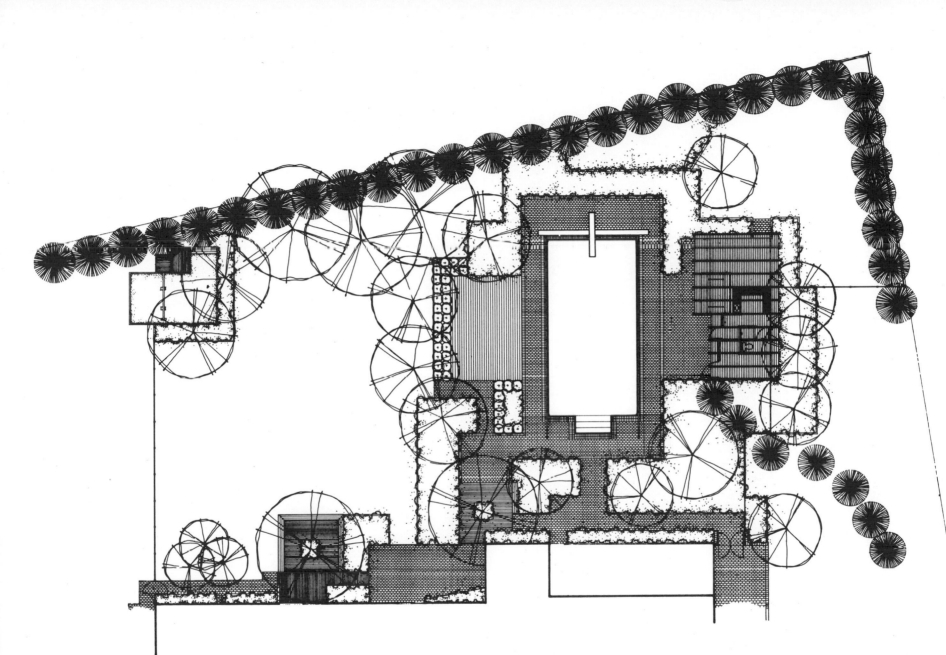

Edmiston residence
1550 Willow Lane

General plan

53

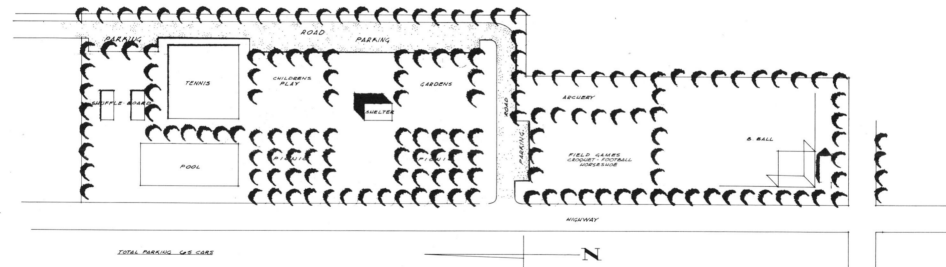

PARKING

ROAD   PARKING

TENNIS

CHILDRENS
PLAY

GARDENS

SHUFFLE-BOARD

SHELTER

ROAD

ARCHERY

PARKING

POOL

PICNIC

PICNIC

FIELD GAMES
CROQUET - FOOTBALL
HORSESHOE

B. BALL

HIGHWAY

TOTAL PARKING 65 CARS

N

CENTRAL CITY PARK STUDIES   1961

54

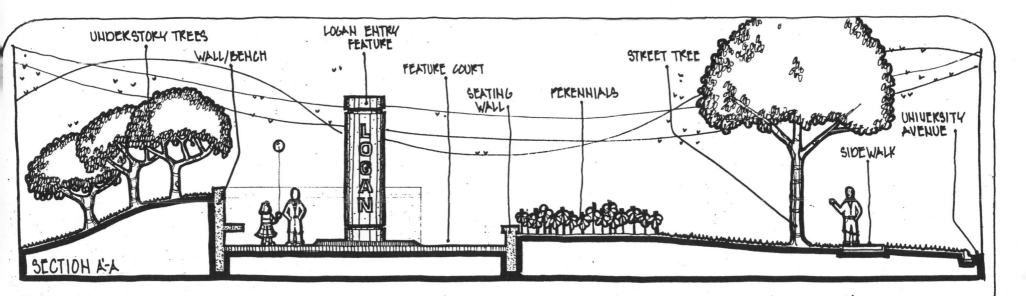

UNDERSTORY TREES
WALL/BENCH
LOGAN ENTRY FEATURE
FEATURE COURT
SEATING WALL
PERENNIALS
STREET TREE
UNIVERSITY AVENUE
SIDEWALK
LOGAN

SECTION A-A

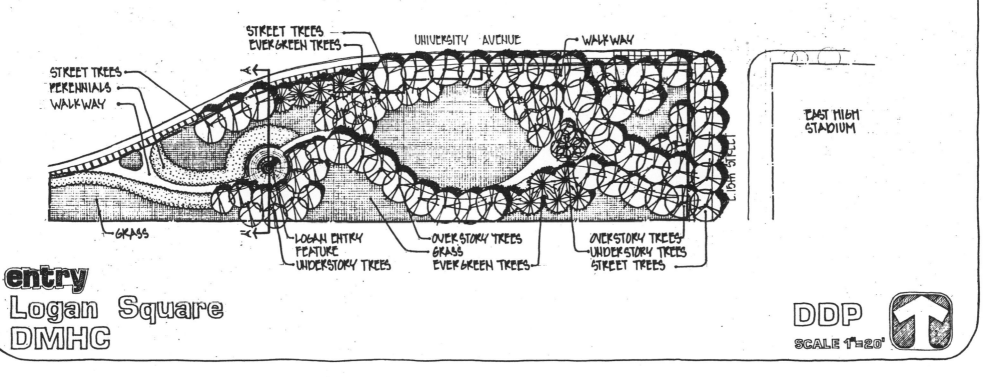

STREET TREES
EVERGREEN TREES
UNIVERSITY AVENUE
WALKWAY

STREET TREES
PERENNIALS
WALKWAY

EAST HIGH STADIUM

E. 16th STREET

GRASS

LOGAN ENTRY FEATURE
UNDERSTORY TREES

OVERSTORY TREES
GRASS
EVERGREEN TREES

OVERSTORY TREES
UNDERSTORY TREES
STREET TREES

entry
Logan Square
DMHC

DDP
SCALE 1"=20'

55

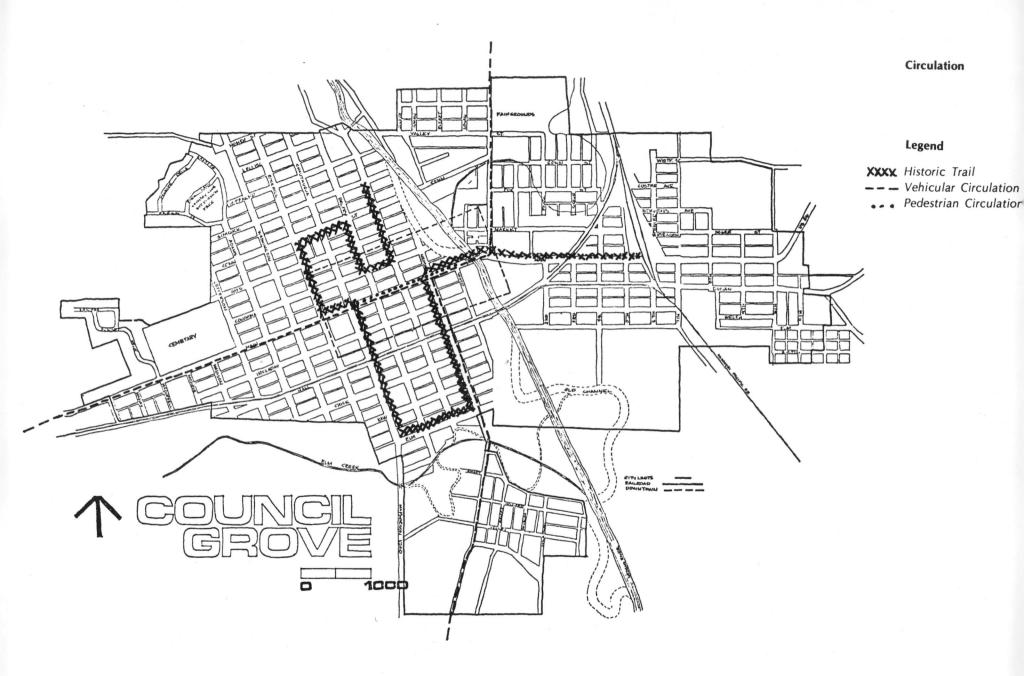

Circulation

Legend

XXXX *Historic Trail*
— — — *Vehicular Circulation*
• • • *Pedestrian Circulation*

CITY LIMITS
RAILROAD
DOWNTOWN

↑ COUNCIL GROVE

0   1000

56

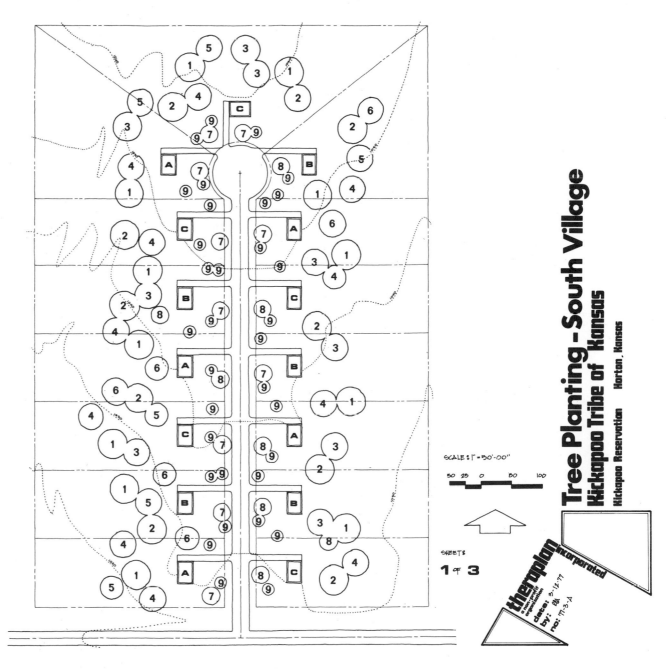

KEY	SCIEN. NAME	COMMON NAME	SIZE/COND'T.	QUANT.
1	PLATANUS OCCIDENTALIS	SYCAMORE	10-12 BB	12
2	GLEDITSIA TRIACANTHOS INV	HONEYLOCUST	10-12 BB	10
3	QUERCUS MACROCARPA	BUR OAK	10-12 BB	9
4	QUERCUS PALUSTRIS	PIN OAK	8-10 BB	11
5	FRAXINUS PENNSYLVANICA	GREEN ASH	8-10 BB	6
6	MORUS RUBRA	FRUITLESS MULB.	8-10 BB	6
7	PINUS SYLVESTRIS	SCOTCH PINE	6-8 BB	10
8	ELEAGNUS ANGUSTIFOLIA	RUSSIAN OLIVE	6-8 BB	8
9	CERCIS CANADENSIS	RED BUD	6-8 BB	33

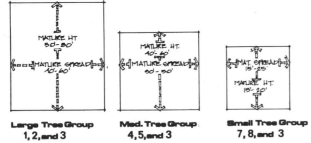

Large Tree Group
1, 2, and 3

Med. Tree Group
4, 5, and 3

Small Tree Group
7, 8, and 3

Residential Plantings:

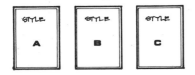

STYLE A   STYLE B   STYLE C

SEE SHEET 3 FOR PLANTING DETAILS

Tree Planting - South Village
Kickapoo Tribe of Kansas
Kickapoo Reservation   Horton, Kansas

SCALE: 1" = 50'-00"

50 25 0   50   100

SHEET:
1 of 3

theraplan
incorporated

date: 3-12-77
by: DjK
no: M-3-A

57

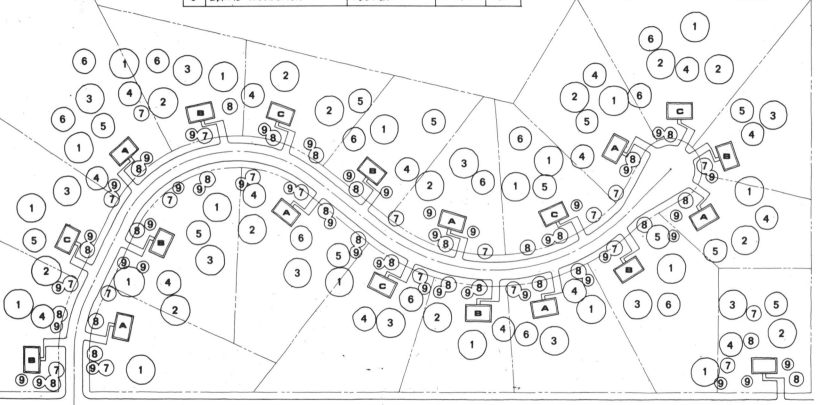

Key#	Scien. Name	Common Name	Size/Condt.	Quant.
1	PLATANUS OCCIDENTALIS	SYCAMORE	10-12' BB	19
2	GLEDITSIA TRIACANTHOS HV	HONEYLOCUST	10-12' BB	13
3	QUERCUS MACROCARPA	BUR OAK	10-12' BB	11
4	QUERCUS PALUSTRIS	PIN OAK	8-10' BB	16
5	FRAXINUS PENNSYLVANICA	GREEN ASH	8-10' BB	11
6	MORUS RUBRA	FRUITLESS MULB.	8-10' BB	12
7	PINUS SYLVESTRIS	SCOTCH PINE	6-8' BB	19
8	ELEAGNUS ANGUSTIFOLIA	RUSSIAN OLIVE	6-8' BB	27
9	CERCIS CANADENSIS	REDBUD	6-8' BB	42

SEE SHEET 3 FOR RESIDENCE DETAIL

Tree Planting North Village
Kickapoo Tribe of Kansas
Kickapoo Reservation   Horton Kansas

SCALE: 1"=50'00"

50 25 0   50   100'

SHEET
2 of 3

theraplan incorporated
a landscape architecture organization
date: 9-12-77
by: BG
no: 17-3-A

58

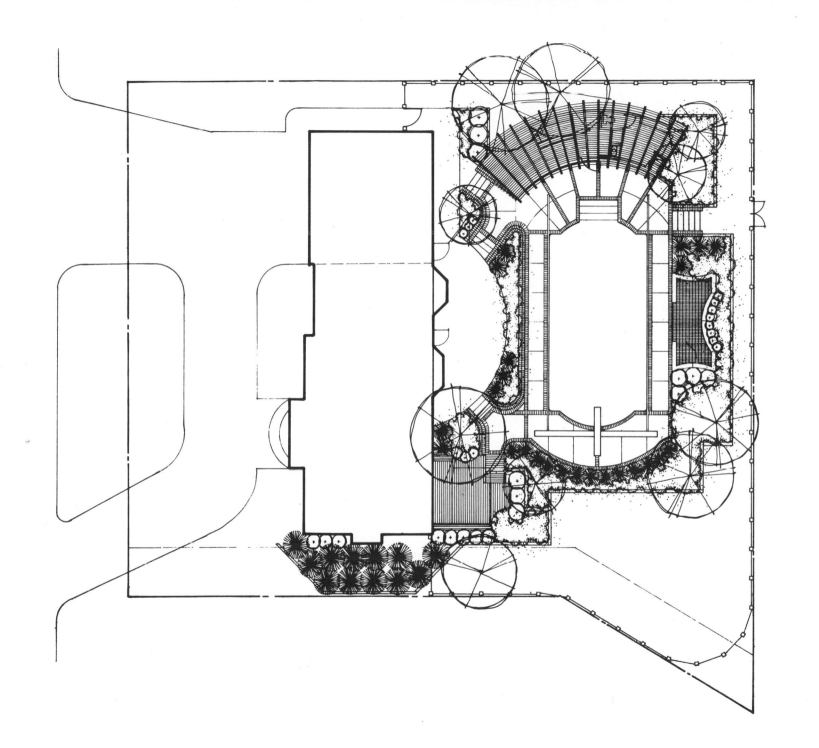

Warren Residence

14215 North Point Blvd.

59

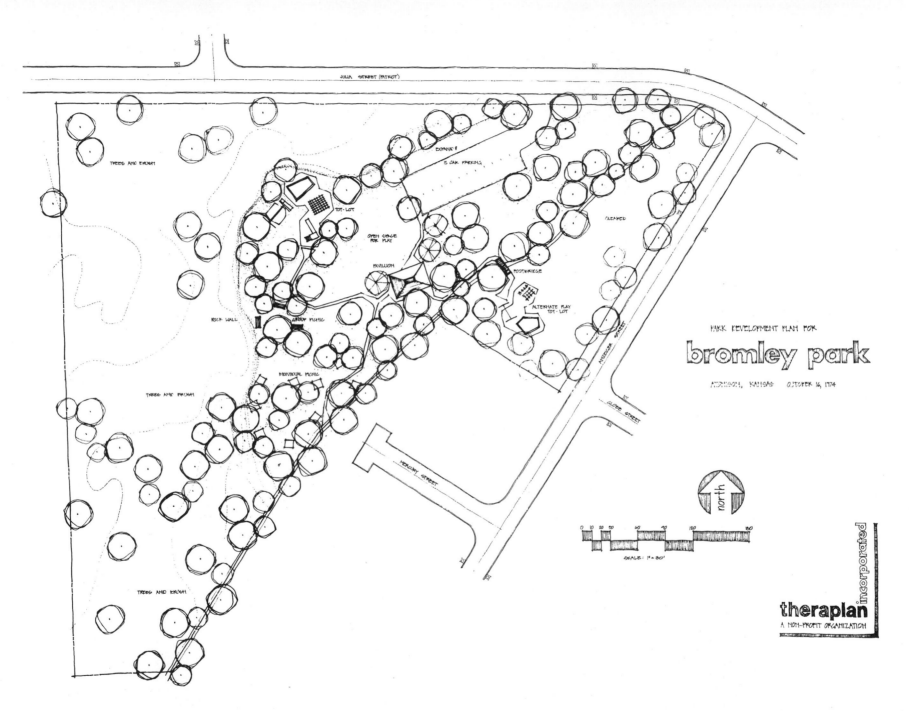

JULIA STREET (PATRIOT)

TREES AND BRUSH

EXPAND ± 15 CAR PARKING

CLEARED

TOT-LOT

OPEN SPACE FOR PLAY

PAVILION

FOOTBRIDGE

ALTERNATE PLAY TOT-LOT

ROCK WALL

ARBOR PICNIC

INDIVIDUAL PICNIC

TREES AND BRUSH

MERCURY STREET

INTERIOR STREET

GLOBE STREET

PARK DEVELOPMENT PLAN FOR

bromley park

ATCHISON, KANSAS   OCTOBER 16, 1974

north

0 10 20 30   40   50   100   150

SCALE: 1" = 30'

TREES AND BRUSH

60

THERE ARE MANY TOOLS AVAILABLE TO REPRESENT THE DESIGN PROGRAM. THE COMPUTER WILL NOT REPLACE THE DESIGNER. IT WILL, HOWEVER, PROVIDE ASSISTANCE IN ILLUSTRATING ALL PHASES OF THE GRAPHIC PROCESS.

COMPUTER

4

Most computer programs are well adapted to the analysis phase of both design and graphic representation. The extensive data base that must be compiled for project implementation can be easily summarized on the printout page. The versatility of scale illustration is also a useable feature of this valuable tool.

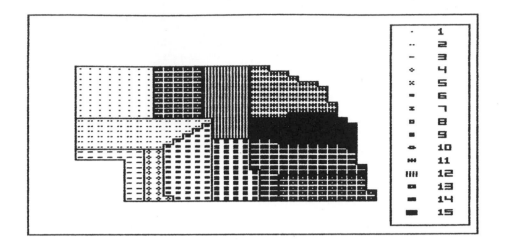

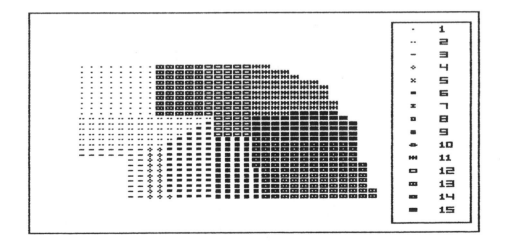

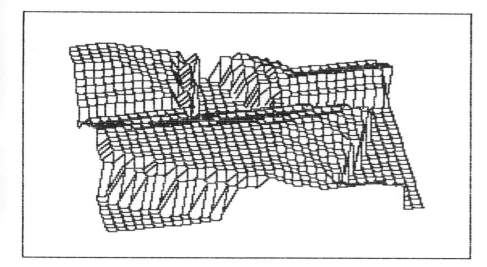

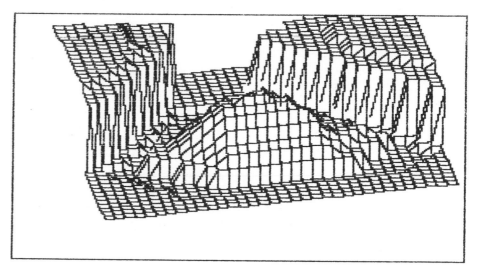

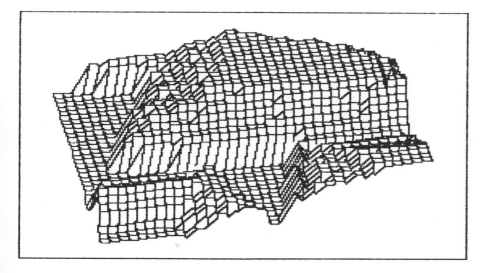

VARIOUS CUT AND FILL ALTERNATIVES ON THE SAME SITE CAN BE ILLUSTRATED ON A SINGLE SHEET WITH THE COMPUTER.

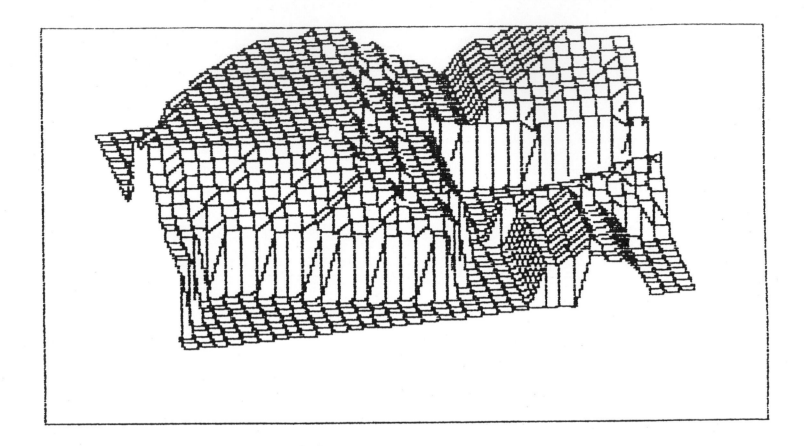

THE ENLARGED SITE PRINTOUT OFFERS THE
CLIENT A UNIQUE PERSPECTIVE OF THE
EXISTING OR PROPOSED ALTERATIONS. WITHOUT
THE PROPER SUPPORT, HOWEVER, ONLY THE
DESIGNER WILL KNOW THE DESIGN OR GRAPHIC
VALUES OF THE SOLUTION.

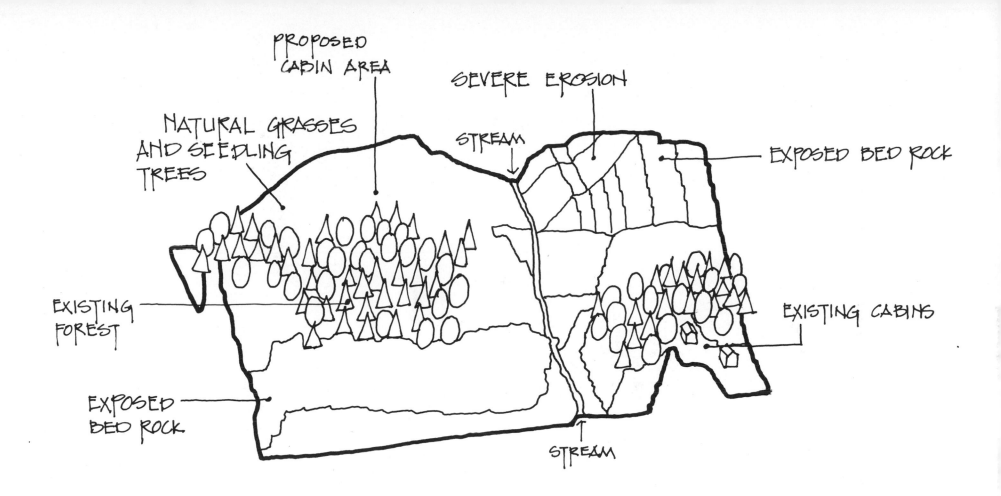

PROPOSED
CABIN AREA

SEVERE EROSION

NATURAL GRASSES
AND SEEDLING
TREES

STREAM

EXPOSED BED ROCK

EXISTING
FOREST

EXISTING CABINS

EXPOSED
BED ROCK

STREAM

THE ARTISTIC QUALITY OF THE COMPUTER
IMAGE CAN BE INHANCED WITH THE USE
OF A FREE-HAND OVERLAY. VARIOUS
DEVELOPMENT ALTERNATIVES CAN BE
SHOWN TO A CLIENT WITHOUT EXTENSIVE
MAPPING.

65

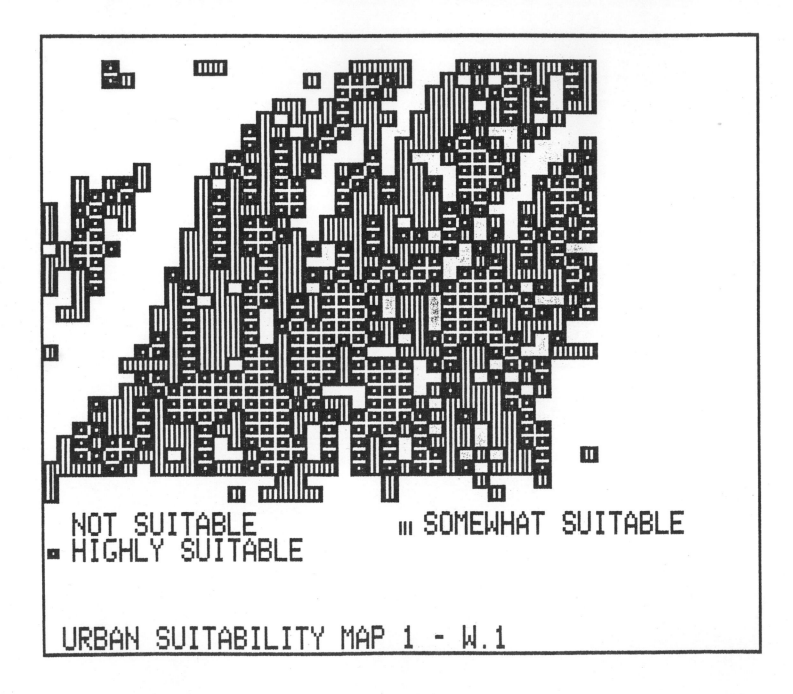

NOT SUITABLE   ⅢSOMEWHAT SUITABLE

■ HIGHLY SUITABLE

URBAN SUITABILITY MAP 1 - W.1

66

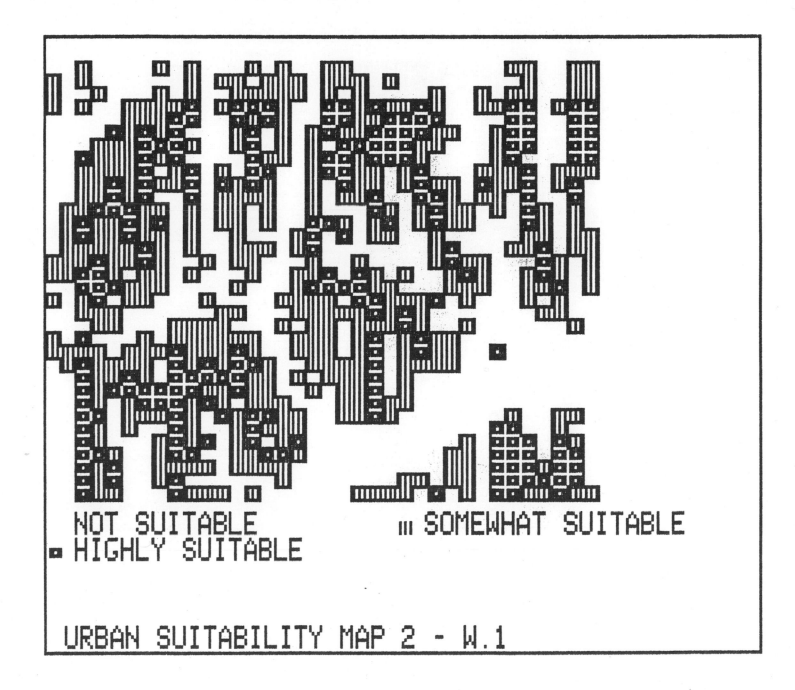

NOT SUITABLE   ⅲ SOMEWHAT SUITABLE
▪ HIGHLY SUITABLE

URBAN SUITABILITY MAP 2 - W.1

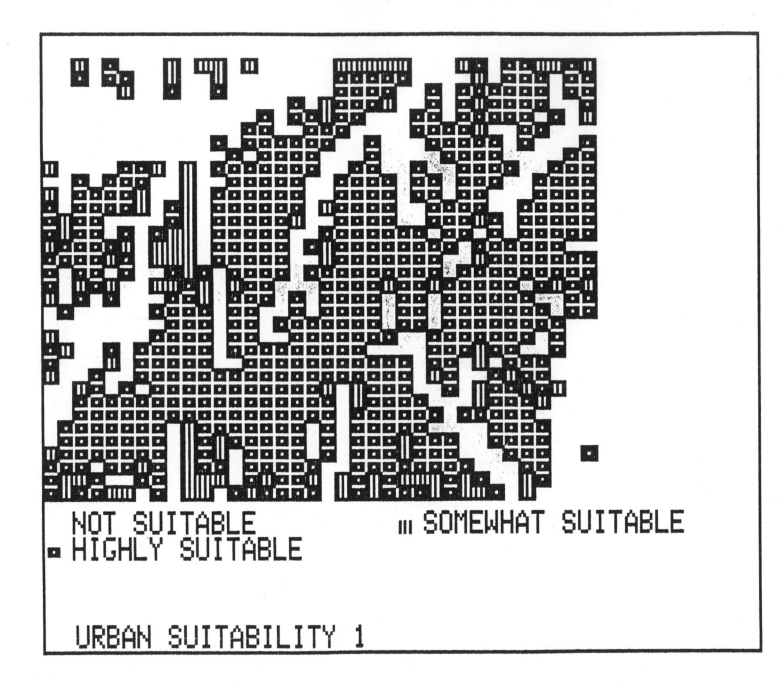

NOT SUITABLE ⫼ SOMEWHAT SUITABLE
▪ HIGHLY SUITABLE

URBAN SUITABILITY 1

68

CR   AR   B   A   C

FRONT ELEVATION "A"

CR   AR   B   A   C

FRONT ELEVATION "B"

Notes

GDS
MCAUTO

Client

Job

Drawing title

Scale | Drawn

Date | Checked

Drawing No | Revision
| 69

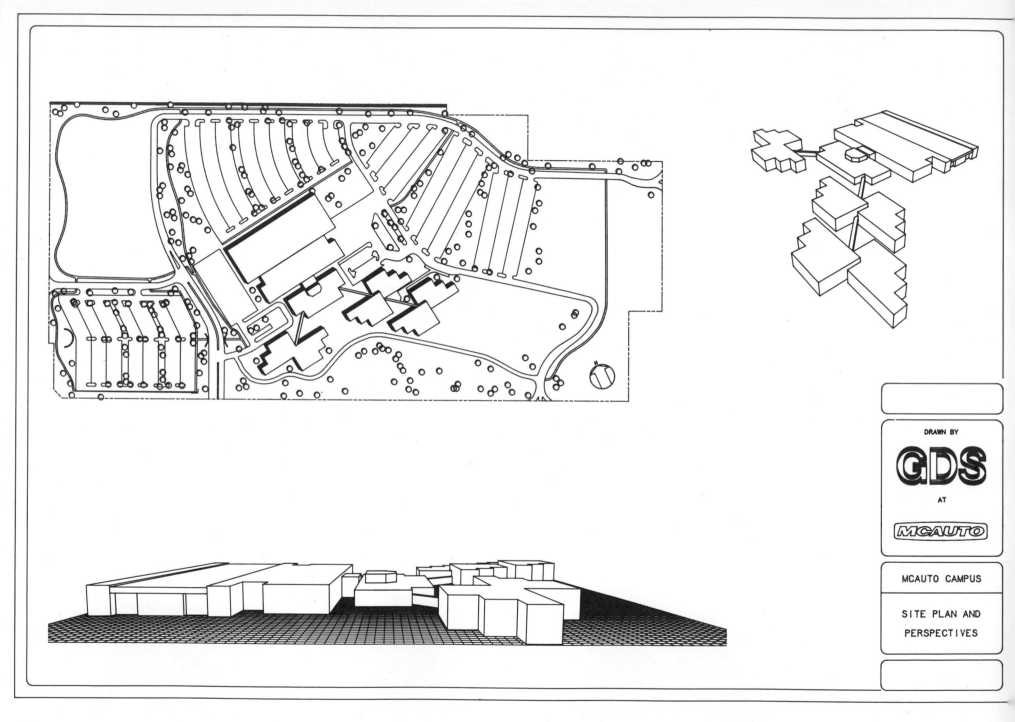

DRAWN BY

GDS

AT

MCAUTO

MCAUTO CAMPUS

SITE PLAN AND
PERSPECTIVES

Once the site plan is completed, it may be necessary to expand the graphics support of the original concepts. Sketches, elevations, and construction drawings should be used to finalize the major issues of the program.

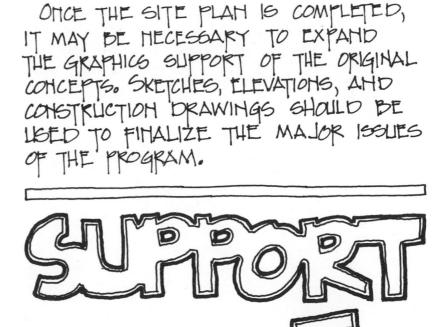

SUPPORT
5

L·A·G

DEVELOPMENT CONCEPT
GRAPHIC TECHNIQUE - PENCIL
1948

72

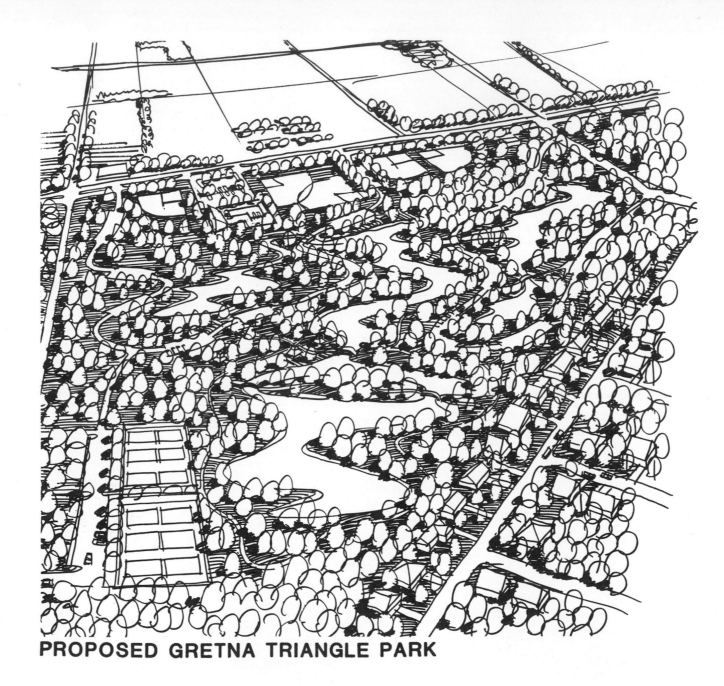

PROPOSED GRETNA TRIANGLE PARK

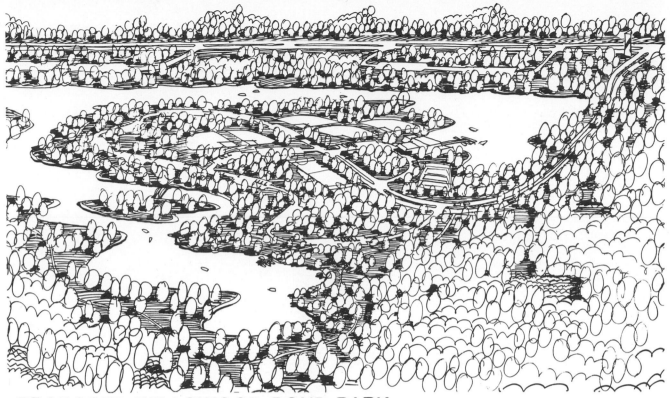

PROPOSED WILLSWOOD POND PARK

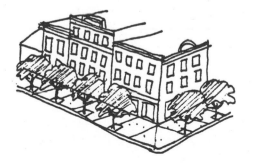

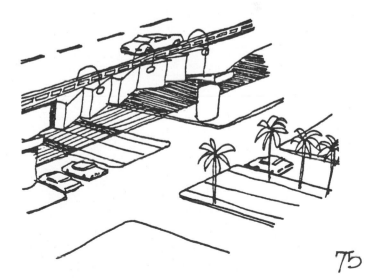

75

CITY HALL

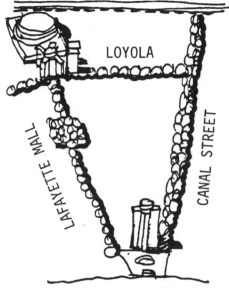

CLAIBORNE AVENUE

LOYOLA

LAFAYETTE MALL

CANAL STREET

RIVER

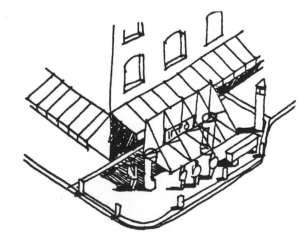

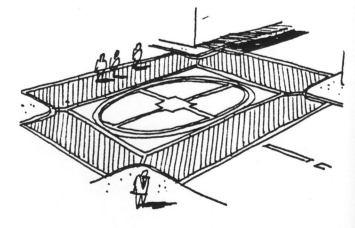

76

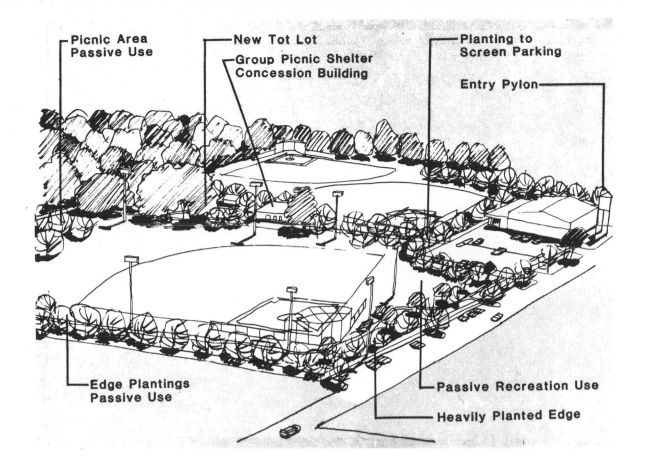

Picnic Area
Passive Use

New Tot Lot

Group Picnic Shelter
Concession Building

Planting to
Screen Parking

Entry Pylon

Edge Plantings
Passive Use

Passive Recreation Use

Heavily Planted Edge

S·1
TYPICAL STREET

S·3
MAJOR PEDESTRIAN STREET

S·2
PEDESTRIAN STREET

M·4

MOBILE INFO UNIT

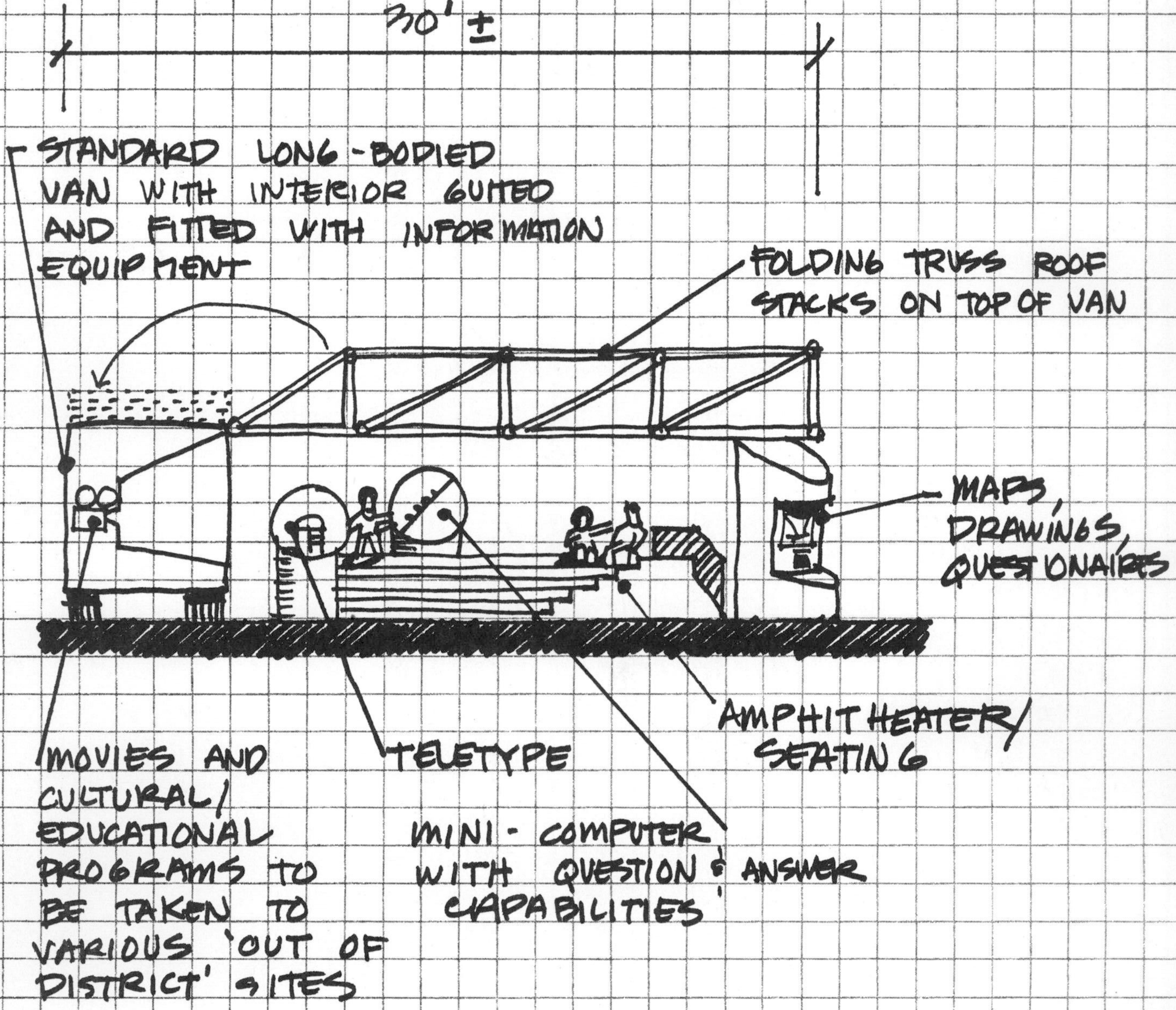

FOLDING TRUSS ROOF STACKS ON TOP OF VAN

MAPS, DRAWINGS, QUESTIONAIRES

AMPHITHEATER/ SEATING

30' ±

STANDARD LONG-BODIED VAN WITH INTERIOR GUTTED AND FITTED WITH INFORMATION EQUIPMENT

TELETYPE

MINI-COMPUTER WITH QUESTION & ANSWER CAPABILITIES

MOVIES AND CULTURAL/ EDUCATIONAL PROGRAMS TO BE TAKEN TO VARIOUS 'OUT OF DISTRICT' SITES

WHERE'S N.O. INFLATABLE

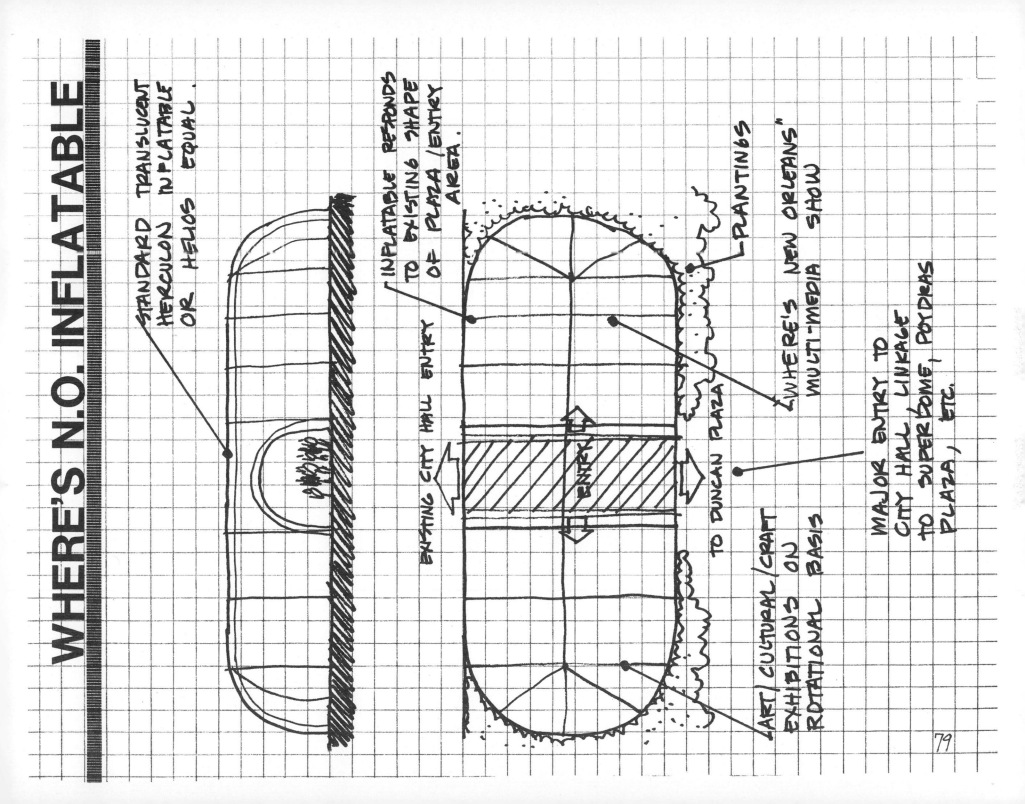

STANDARD TRANSLUCENT HERCULON INFLATABLE OR HELIOS EQUAL.

INFLATABLE RESPONDS TO EXISTING SHAPE OF PLAZA/ENTRY AREA.

PLANTINGS

"WHERE'S NEW ORLEANS" MULTI-MEDIA SHOW

EXISTING CITY HALL ENTRY

ENTRY

TO DUNCAN PLAZA

MAJOR ENTRY TO CITY HALL LINKAGE TO SUPERDOME, POYDRAS PLAZA, ETC.

ART/CULTURAL/CRAFT EXHIBITIONS ON ROTATIONAL BASIS

79

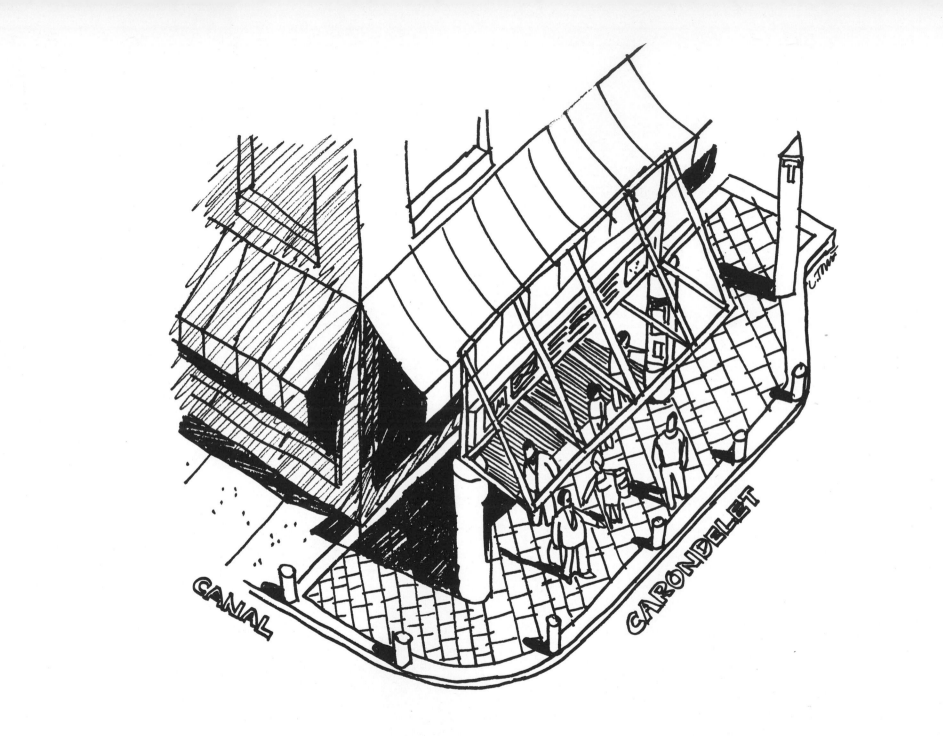

CANAL

CARONDELET

80

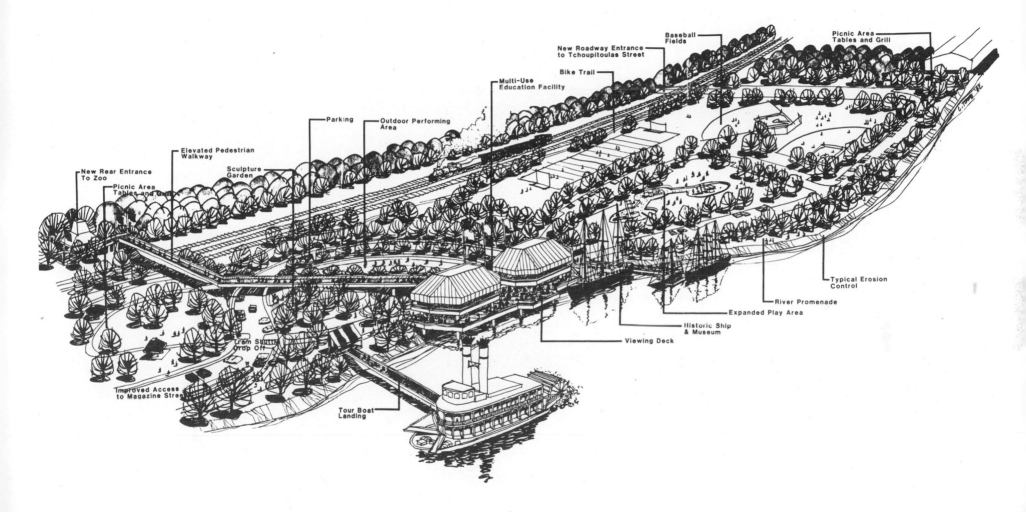

New Rear Entrance
To Zoo

Picnic Area
Tables and Grill

Elevated Pedestrian
Walkway

Sculpture
Garden

Parking

Outdoor Performing
Area

Multi-Use
Education Facility

New Roadway Entrance
to Tchoupitoulas Street

Bike Trail

Baseball
Fields

Picnic Area
Tables and Grill

Typical Erosion
Control

River Promenade

Expanded Play Area

Historic Ship
& Museum

Viewing Deck

Tram Shuttle
Drop Off

Improved Access
to Magazine Street

Tour Boat
Landing

83

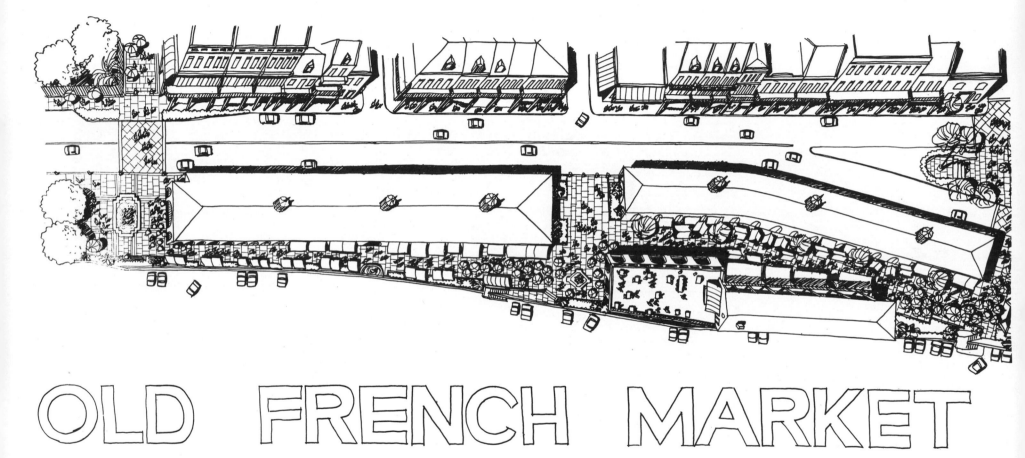

OLD FRENCH MARKET

C.R.C.

EXTERIOR PERSPECTIVE

85

DESIGN 440
R.E. CUNNINGHAM

86

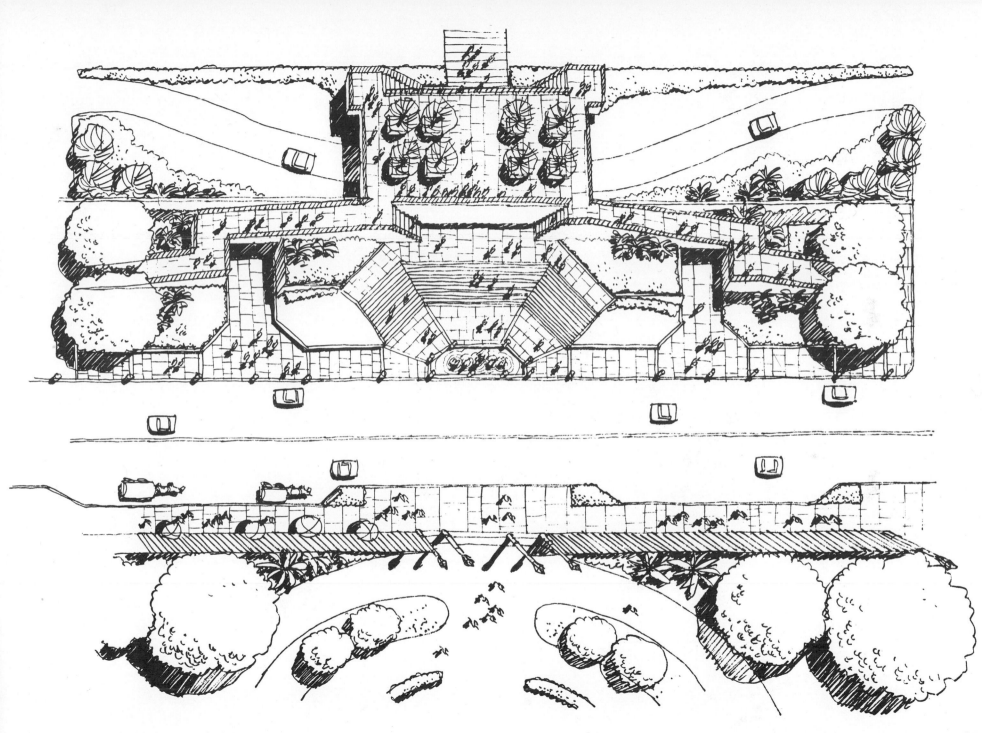

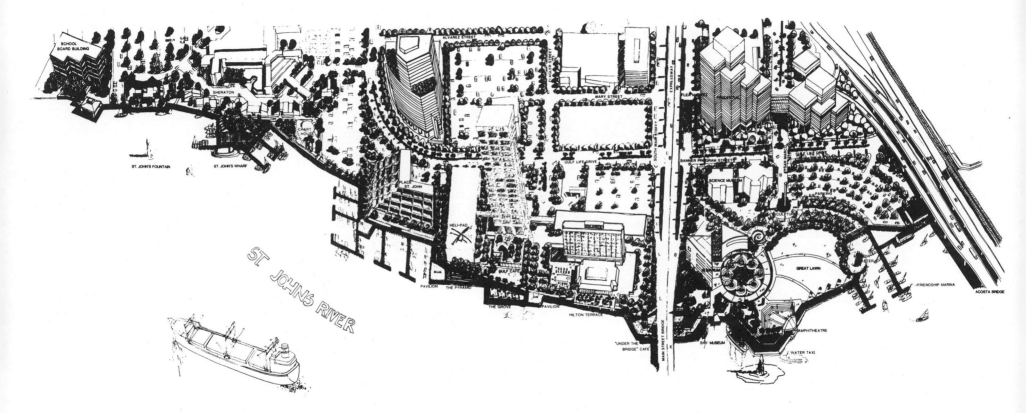

SCHOOL
BOARD BUILDING

ST. JOHN'S FOUNTAIN

SHERATON

COURT
HOUSE

ST. JOHN'S WHARF

ALVAREZ STREET

FLAGLER STREET

MARY STREET

EXPRESSWAY

SOUTH MAIN STREET

GULF LIFE DRIVE

BANNER PROGRAM STREET

PLACE
ST. JOHN

SCIENCE MUSEUM

HELI-PAD

PARKING

SCULPTURE

GULF CAFE

GREAT LAWN

ST. JOHN'S RIVER

PAVILION   THE PYRAMID

FRIENDSHIP MARINA

THE GROVE   PAVILION

ACOSTA BRIDGE

HILTON TERRACE

"UNDER THE
BRIDGE" CAFE

MAIN STREET BRIDGE

SHIP MUSEUM

AMPHITHEATRE

WATER TAXI

88

LANDSCAPE CONCEPT
PEN AND INK
1925

89

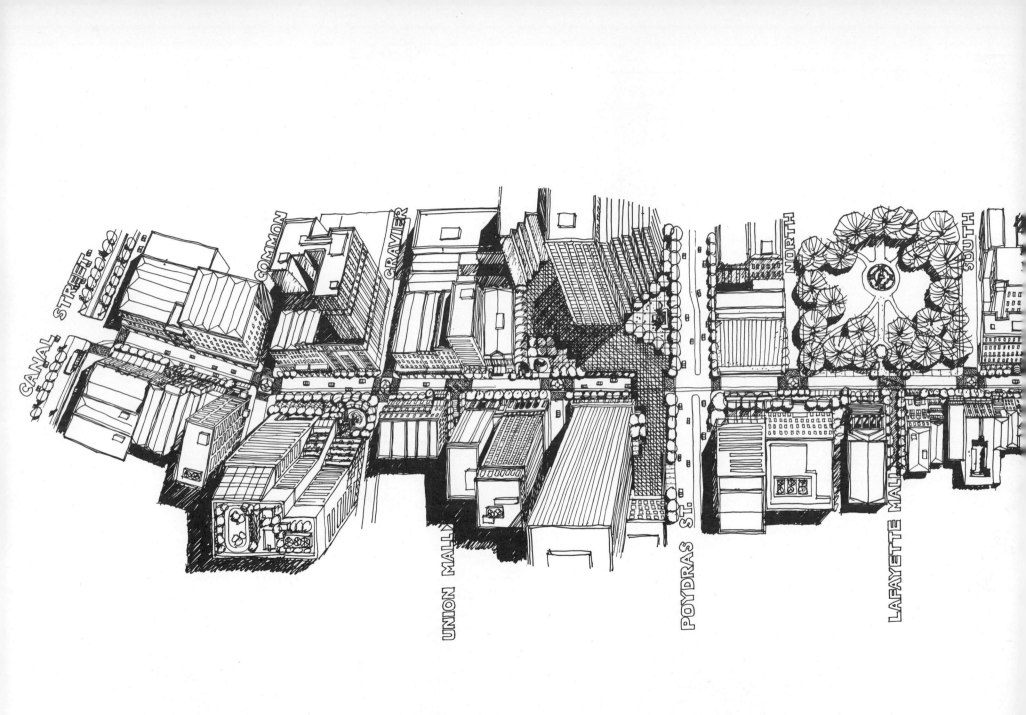

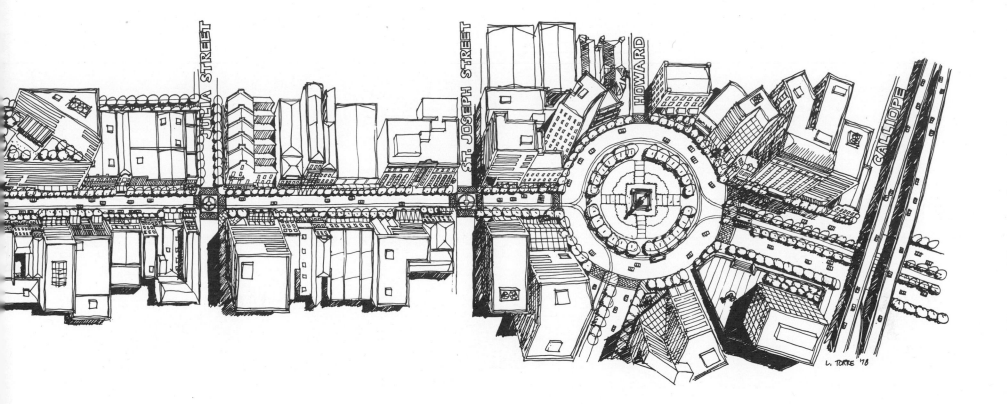

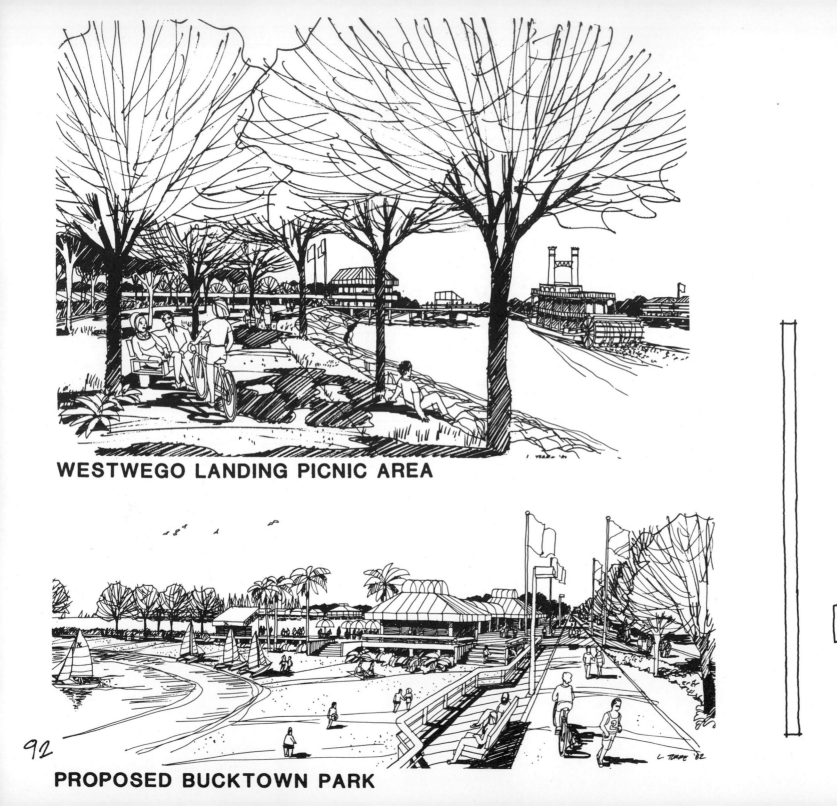

WESTWEGO LANDING PICNIC AREA

PROPOSED BUCKTOWN PARK

92

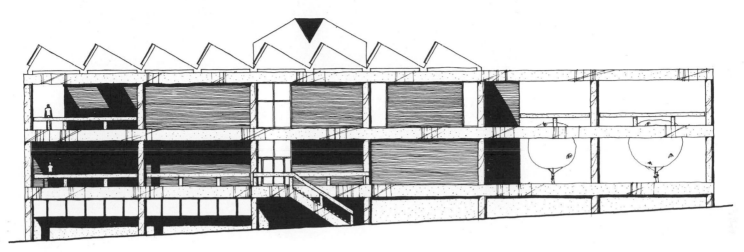

east

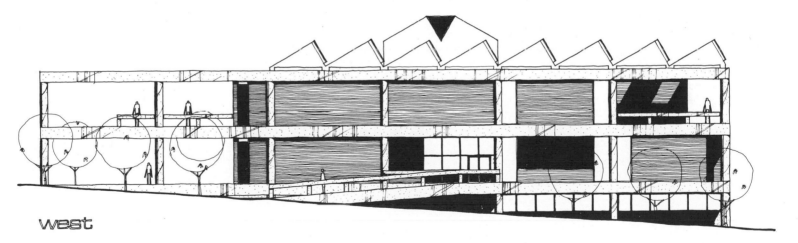

west

elevations

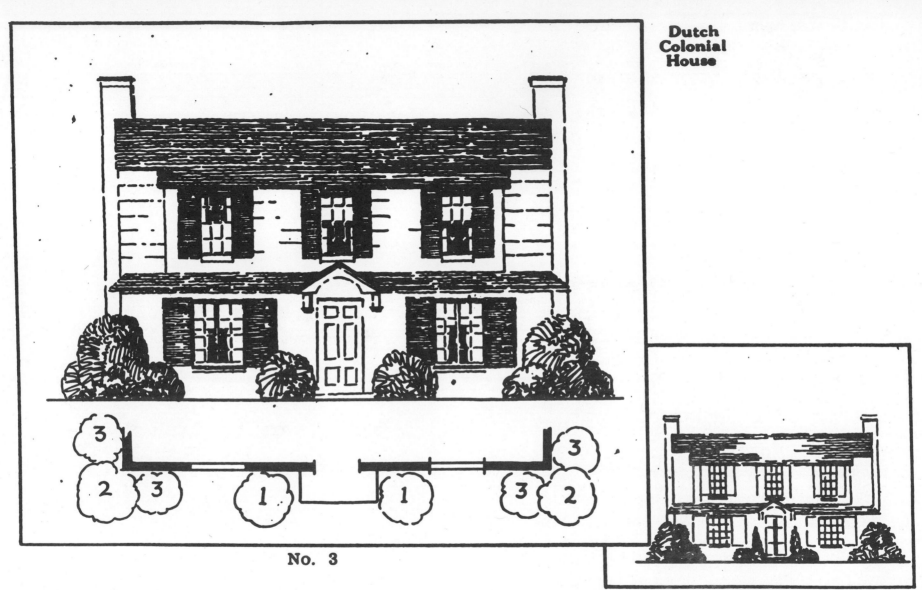

Dutch Colonial House

No. 3

No. 3A

PLANTING CONCEPT
PEN AND INK
1932

94

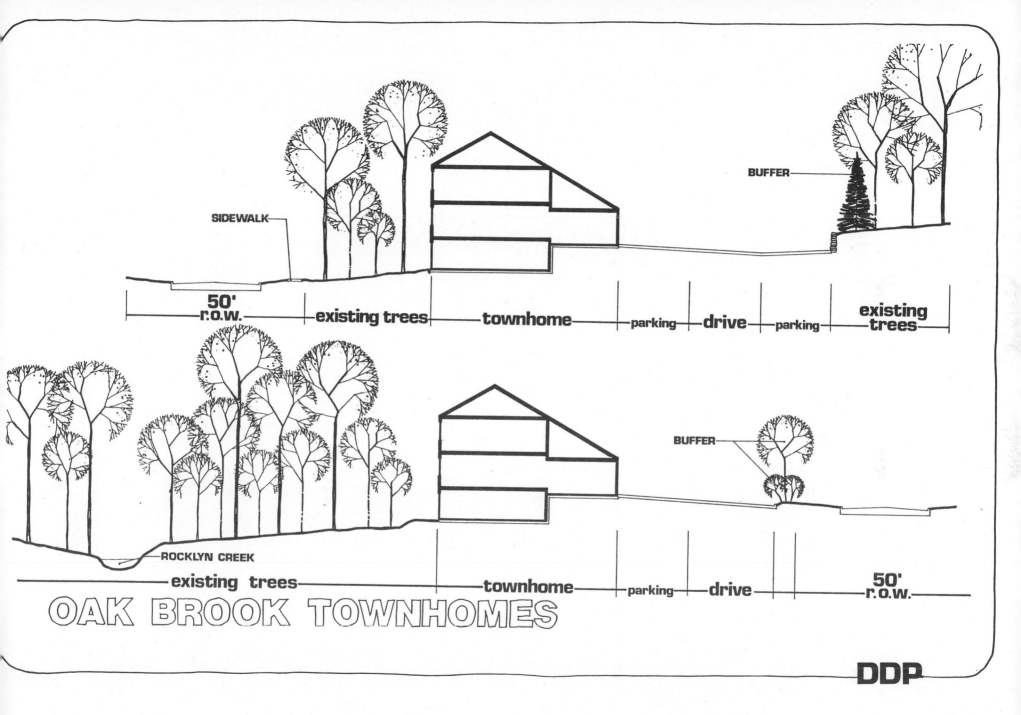

SIDEWALK

50'
r.o.w. — existing trees — townhome — parking — drive — parking — existing trees

BUFFER

ROCKLYN CREEK

existing trees — townhome — parking — drive — 50'
r.o.w.

BUFFER

OAK BROOK TOWNHOMES

DDP

95

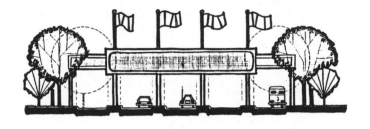

ENTRY   CANOPY

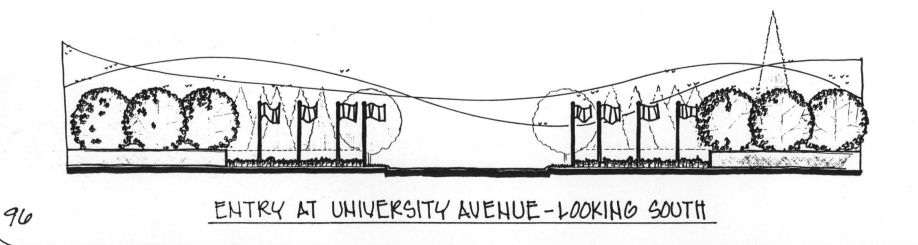

ENTRY AT UNIVERSITY AVENUE - LOOKING SOUTH

LAYOUT AND
GRADING
PLANS

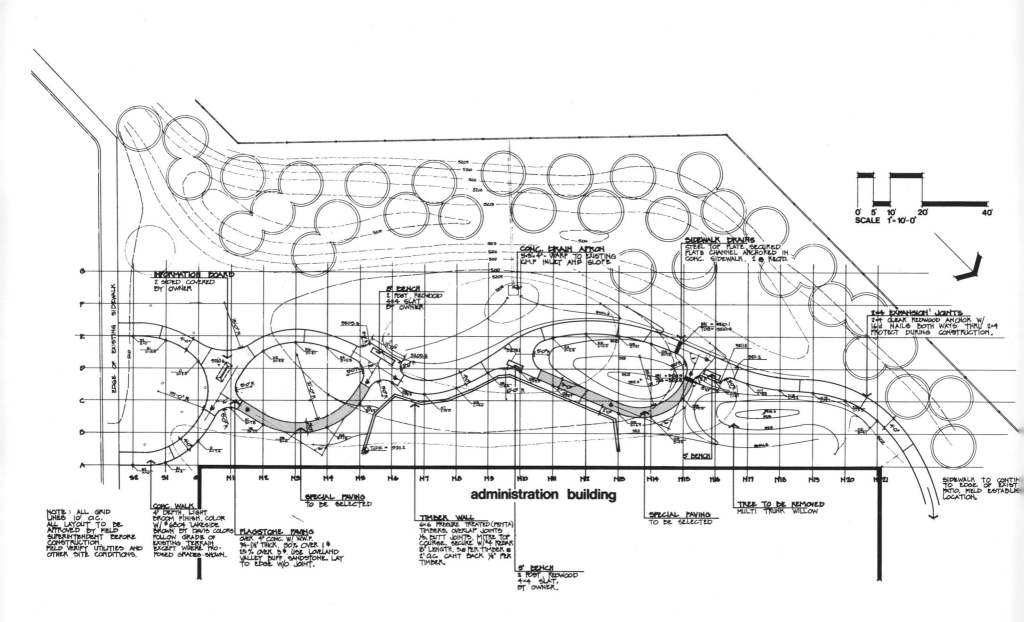

administration building

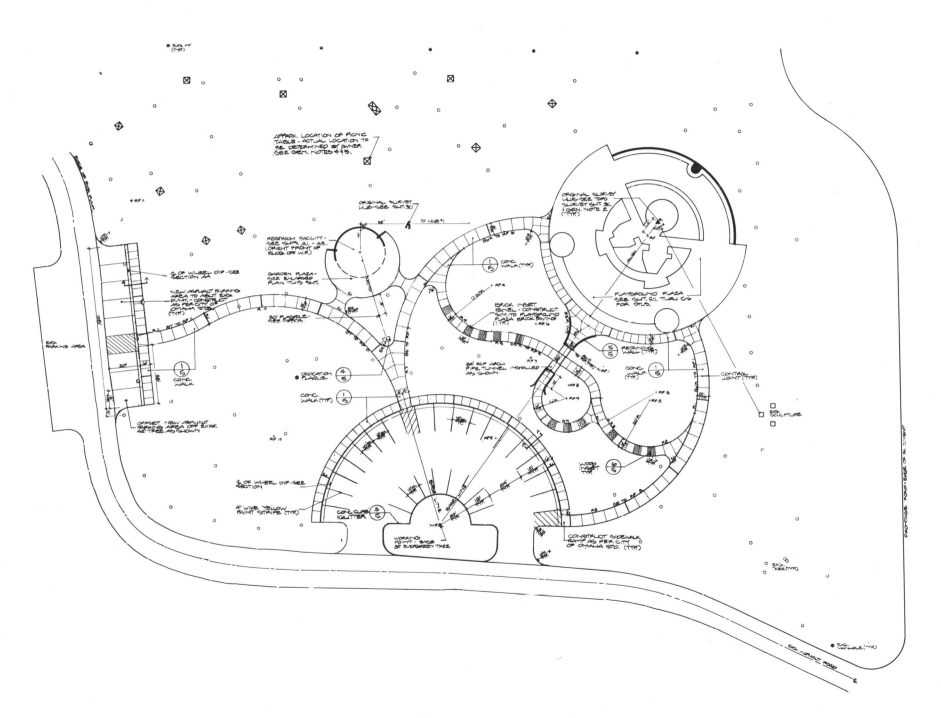

99

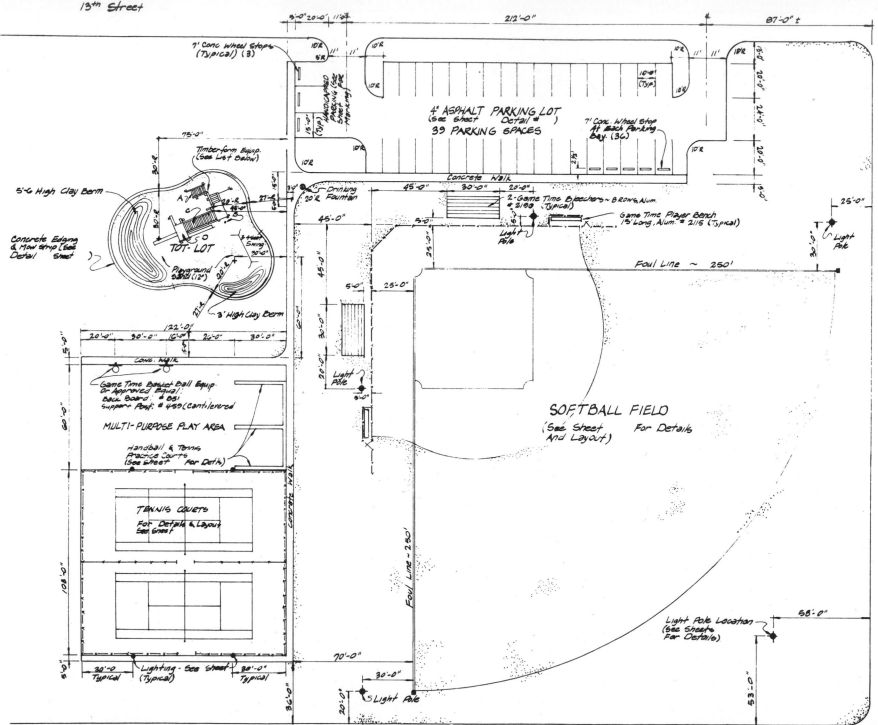

13th Street

5'-0" 20'-0" 11'-0"   212'-0"   87'-0" ±

7' Conc Wheel Stops
(Typical) (3)

HANDICAPPED
PARKING (See
Sheet Pg
Marking)

4" ASPHALT PARKING LOT
(See Sheet   Detail #   )
39 PARKING SPACES

7' Conc. Wheel Stop
At Each Parking
Bay. (36)

10'-0"
(Typ)

10'R
11' 11' 10'R   10'R   10'R 18'R

5'R

15'-0"
20'-0"
20'-0"
24'-0"
5'-0"

Timberform Equip.
(See List Below)

75'-0"

5'-6 High Clay Berm

Concrete Edging
& Mow Strip (See
Detail Sheet)

TOT-LOT

3' High Clay Berm

Playground
Sand (12")

Concrete Walk

Drinking
Fountain

2-Game Time Bleachers ~ 8 ROWS Alum.
2100 (Typical)

Game Time Player Bench
13' Long, Alum. # 2115 (Typical)

45'-0" 30'-0" 20'-0"

45'-0"

25'-0"

Light
Pole

25'-0"   Light
Pole

Foul Line ~ 250'

45'-0"

5'-0" 25'-0"

122'-0"

20'-0" 30'-0" 16'-0" 26'-0" 30'-0"

5'-0"

Conc. Walk

Game Time Basket Ball Equip.
Or Approved Equal:
Back Board : # 851
Support Post : # 459 (Cantilevered)

MULTI-PURPOSE PLAY AREA

Handball & Tennis
Practice Courts
(See Sheet   For Detls)

TENNIS COURTS

For Details & Layout
See Sheet

60'-0"

101'-0"

Light
Pole

SOFTBALL FIELD

(See Sheet   For Details
And Layout)

25'-0" Light
Pole

Light Pole Location
(See Sheets
For Details)

58'-0"

53'-0"

Lighting - See Sheet
(Typical)

30'-0"
Typical

30'-0"
Typical

5'-0"

5'-0"

36'-0"

70'-0"

30'-0"

20'-0" Light Pole

Foul Line ~ 250'

Foul Line ~ 250'

100

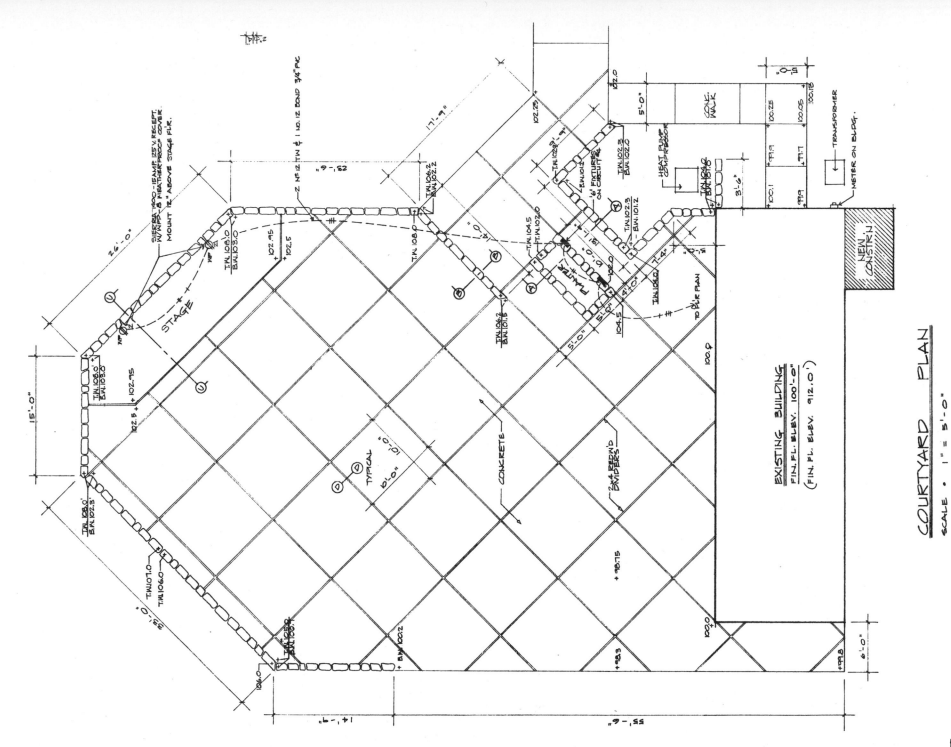

COURTYARD PLAN

SCALE · 1" = 5'-0"

101

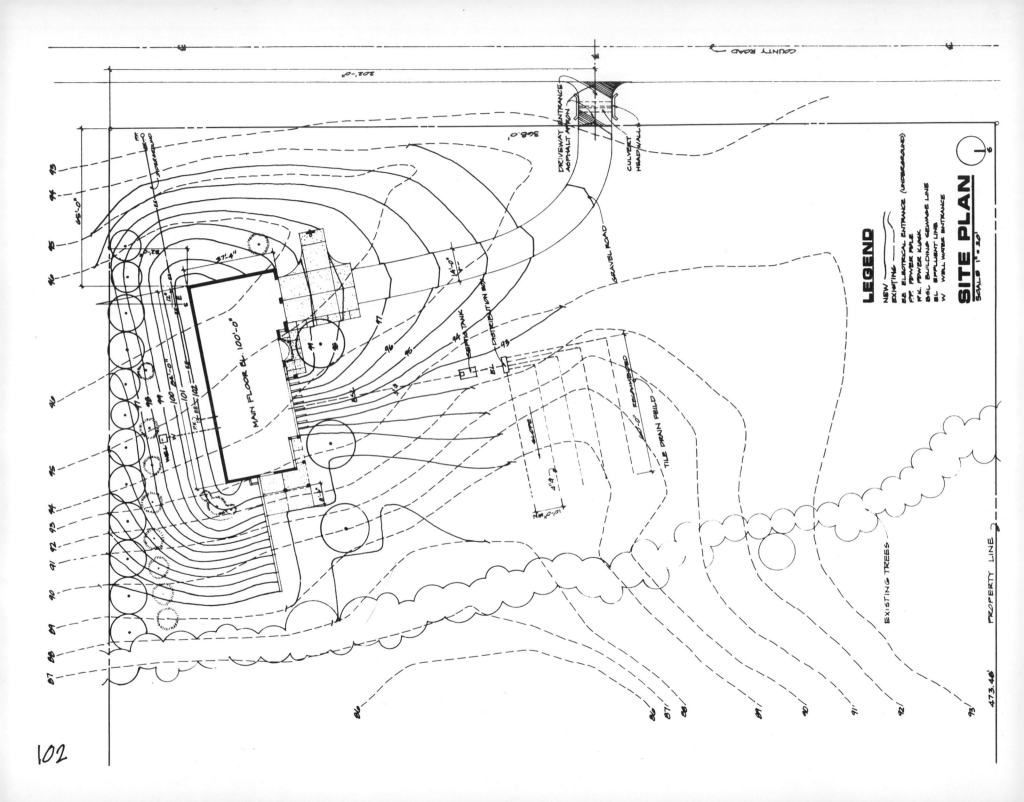

SITE PLAN
SCALE 1" = 20'

LEGEND

NEW _____
EXISTING - - - - - - -
EE ELECTRICAL ENTRANCE (UNDERGROUND)
PP POWER POLE
PK POWER KIOSK
BSL BUILDING SEWAGE LINE
EL EFFLUENT LINE
W   WELL WATER ENTRANCE

MAIN FLOOR EL. 100'-0"

EXISTING TREES

PROPERTY LINE

TILE DRAIN FIELD

SEPTIC TANK

DISTRIBUTION BOX

GRAVEL ROAD

DRIVEWAY ENTRANCE
ASPHALT APRON

CULVERT
HEADWALL

COUNTY ROAD

473.46'

102

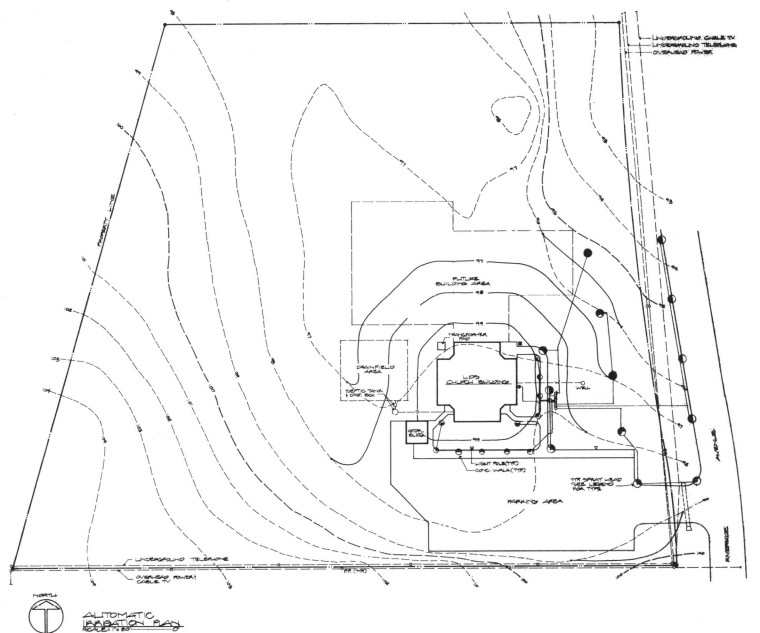

UNDERGROUND CABLE TV
UNDERGROUND TELEPHONE
OVERHEAD POWER

FUTURE
BUILDING AREA

TRANSFORMER
PAD

DRAINFIELD
AREA

SEPTIC TANK
& DIST. BOX

LDS
CHURCH BUILDING

WELL

STOR. BLDG.

LIGHT POLE (TYP.)
CONC. WALK (TYP.)

TYP. SPRAY HEAD
SEE LEGEND
FOR TYPE

PARKING AREA

UNDERGROUND TELEPHONE
OVERHEAD POWER &
CABLE TV

NORTH

AUTOMATIC
IRRIGATION PLAN
SCALE 1"=20'

MATERIAL & EQUIPMENT		
ITEM	DESCRIPTION	APPROX. QTY.
	TORO SERIES S-600 F ROTARY HEAD	2
	TORO SERIES S-600 FC ROTARY HEAD	6
	TORO SERIES S-600 HC ROTARY HEAD	5
	TORO SERIES 570F-15-H	6
	TORO SERIES 570F-15-Q	3
	TORO PRESSURE VACUUM BREAKER MODEL PVB 1"	1
	TORO SERIES 630 ELEC VALVE-1" (IN BOX)	8
	SCHEDULE 40 PVC PIPE AS SPEC.	810 LF.
	CONTROLLER: TORO IC-8 SERIES SOLID STATE-INDOOR	1

NOTES:
1. ALL MATERIALS & EQUIPMENT SHALL BE INSTALLED AS PER MANUFACTURER'S RECOMMENDATIONS AND SHALL MEET ALL LOCAL CODE REQUIREMENTS.
2. BACKFILL & TAMP ALL EXCAVATIONS TO ELIMINATE SETTLEMENT.
3. CONTRACTOR SHALL VERIFY THE LOCATION OF ALL UTILITIES PRIOR TO INSTALLATION OF SYSTEM. ANY DAMAGE TO SUCH SHALL BE SOLEY HIS RESPONSIBILITY.

103

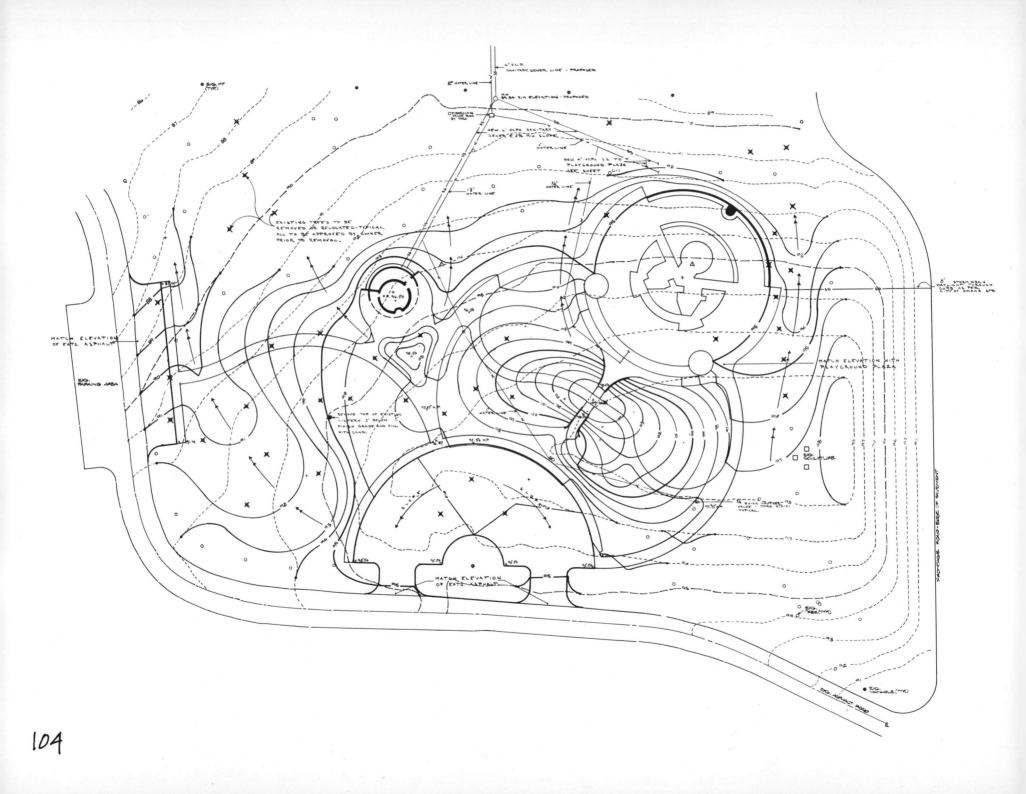

104

THIS SECTION EXHIBITS THE SPECIAL
PRESENTATION TECHNIQUES THAT MAY
BE USED BY A DESIGNER TO EXPAND
DESIGN COMMUNICATIONS. THE REVERSED
GRAPHICS ARE AN EXAMPLE OF
TYPICAL PLANS USED IN A UNIQUE
FORMAT FOR GREATER VISUAL IMPACT.

SPECIAL

6

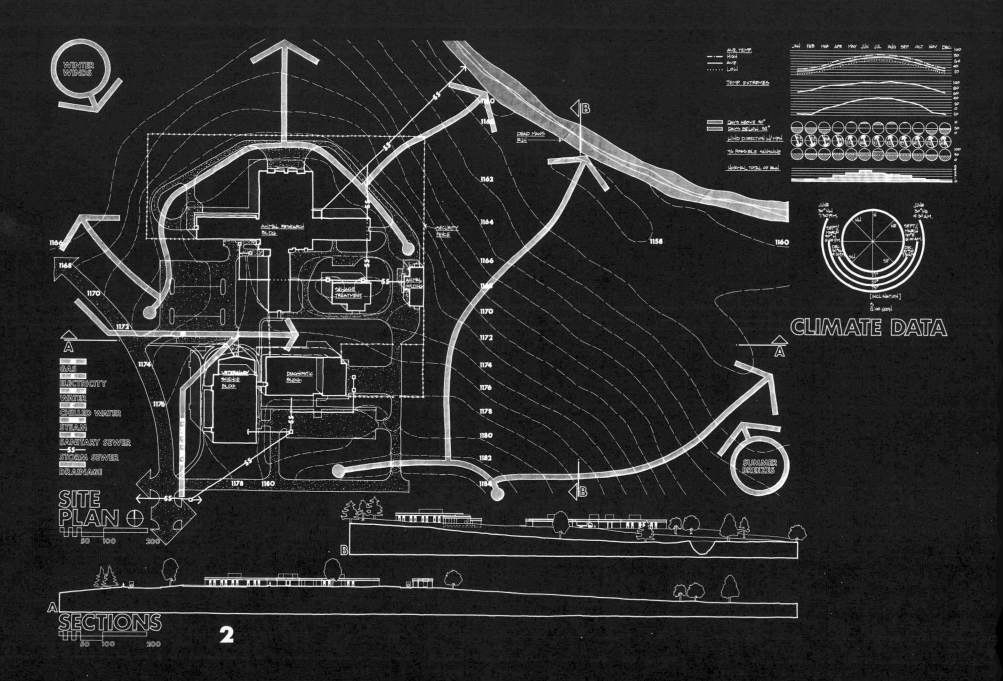

WINTER WINDS

SITE PLAN ⊕

GAS
ELECTRICITY
WATER
CHILLED WATER
STEAM
SANITARY SEWER
STORM SEWER
DRAINAGE

50   100   200

SECTIONS

50   100   200

2

ANIMAL RESEARCH BLDG.

SECURITY FENCE

DEAD MANS RUN

SEWAGE TREATMENT

ANIMAL HOLDING

VETERINARY SCIENCE BLDG.

DIAGNOSTIC BLDG.

1156
1168
1170
1172
1174
1176
1178
1180

1160
1162
1164
1166
1168
1170
1172
1174
1176
1178
1180
1182
1184

1158
1160

SUMMER BREEZES

AVE. TEMP
HIGH
AVE.
LOW

TEMP. EXTREMES

DAYS ABOVE 90°
DAYS BELOW 32°

WIND DIRECTION W/ MPH

% POSSIBLE SUNSHINE

NORMAL TOTAL OF RAIN

JAN FEB MAR APR MAY JUN JUL AUG SEP OCT NOV DEC

JUNE 30 NW 7:30 PM.

JUNE 30 NE 9:30 A.M.

SEPT/ MAR 21 6:00 PM.

SEPT/ MAR 21 6:00 A.M.

DEC 30 SW 4:30 PM.

DEC 30 SE 7:30 A.M.

[INCLINATION]

12:00 NOON

CLIMATE DATA

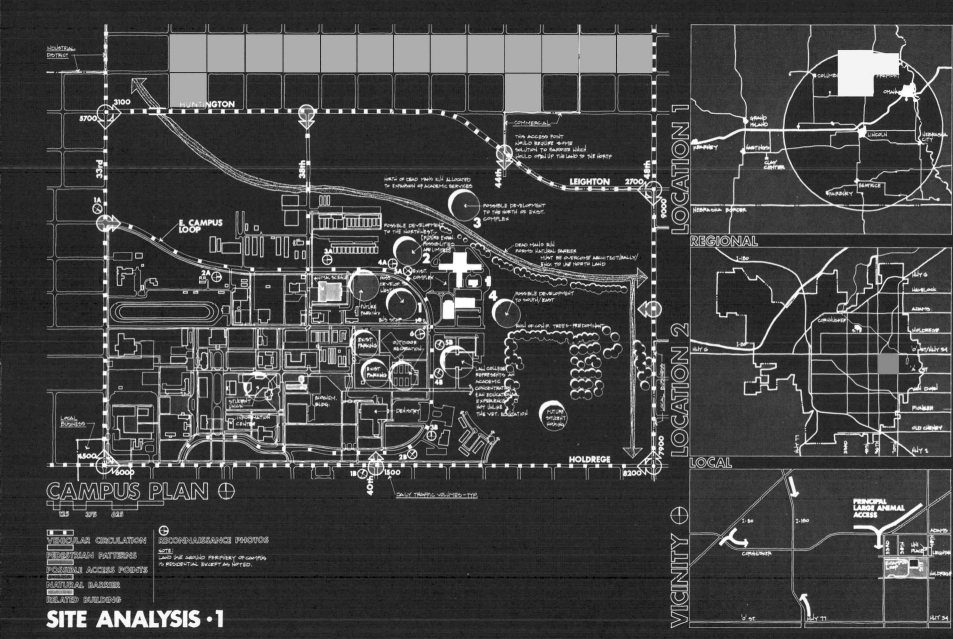

SITE ANALYSIS · 1

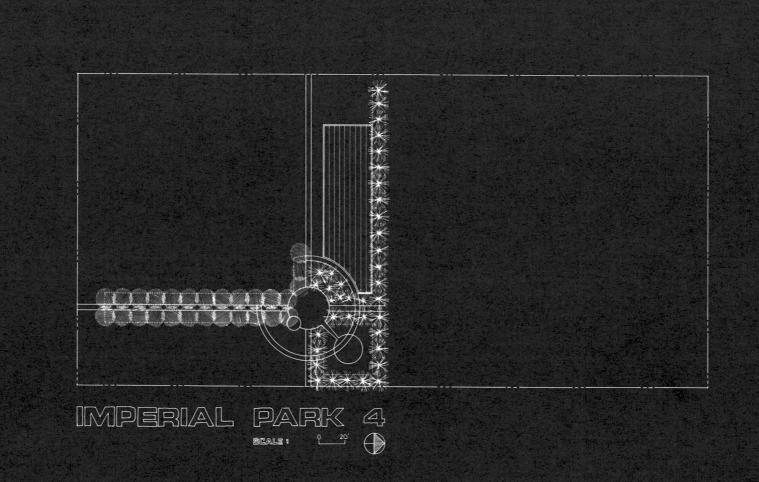

IMPERIAL PARK 4

SCALE: 0 20'

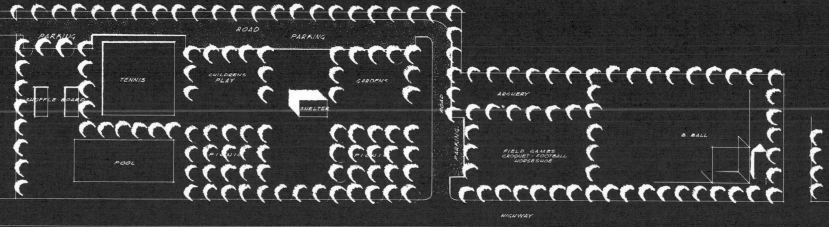

PARKING ROAD PARKING

TENNIS CHILDRENS PLAY GARDENS

SHUFFLE BOARD SHELTER ARCHERY

ROAD

POOL PICNIC PICNIC FIELD GAMES
CROQUET - FOOTBALL
HORSESHOE B. BALL

PARKING

HIGHWAY

TOTAL PARKING 65 CARS

N

CENTRAL CITY PARK STUDIES 1961

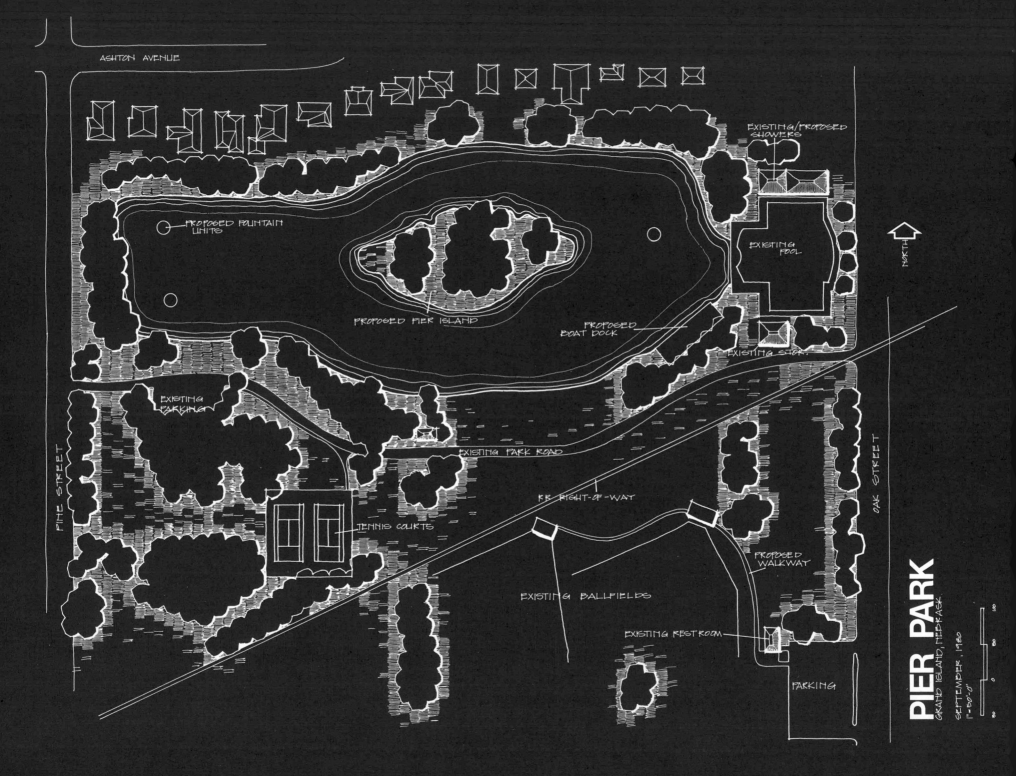

ASHTON AVENUE

EXISTING/PROPOSED
SHOWERS

PROPOSED FOUNTAIN
UNITS

NORTH

EXISTING
POOL

PROPOSED PIER ISLAND

PROPOSED
BOAT DOCK

EXISTING STOR.

EXISTING
PARKING

PINE STREET

EXISTING PARK ROAD

RR RIGHT-OF-WAY

OAK STREET

TENNIS COURTS

PROPOSED
WALKWAY

EXISTING BALLFIELDS

EXISTING RESTROOM

PARKING

PIER PARK

GRAND ISLAND, NEBRASK

SEPTEMBER, 1980

1"=50'-0"

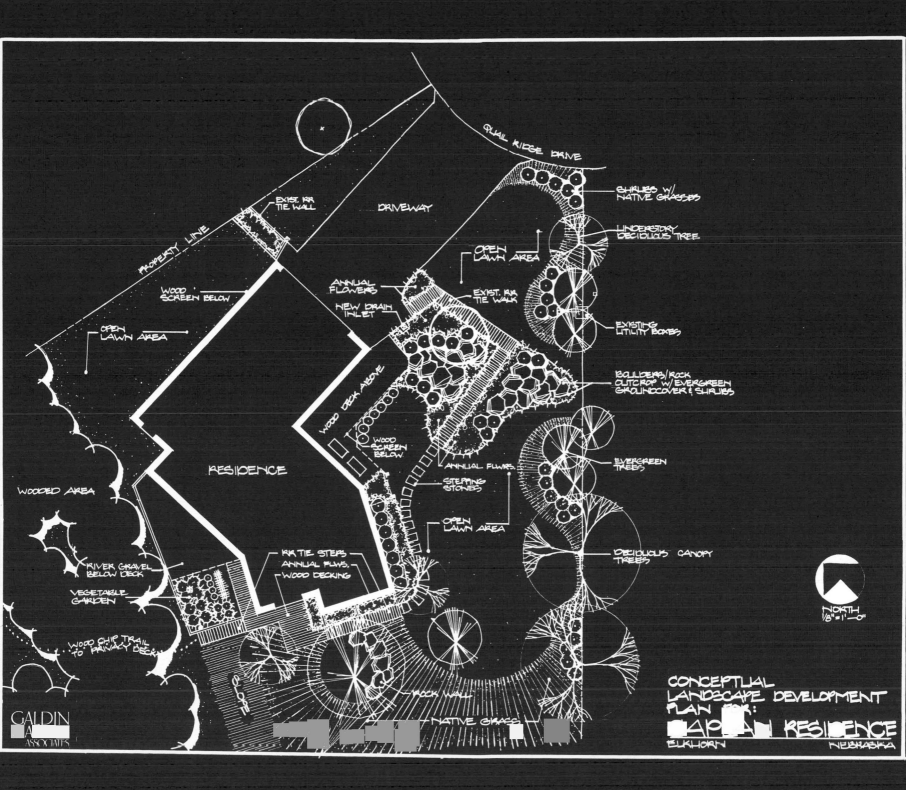

EXIST. RR
TIE WALL

DRIVEWAY

QUAIL RIDGE DRIVE

PROPERTY LINE

SHRUBS W/
NATIVE GRASSES

UNDERSTORY
DECIDUOUS TREE

WOOD
SCREEN BELOW

OPEN
LAWN AREA

OPEN
LAWN AREA

EXIST. RR
TIE WALK

EXISTING
UTILITY BOXES

ANNUAL
FLOWERS

NEW DRAIN
INLET

BOULDERS/ROCK
OUTCROP W/ EVERGREEN
GROUNDCOVER & SHRUBS

WOOD DECK ABOVE

RESIDENCE

WOOD
SCREEN
BELOW

ANNUAL FLWRS.

EVERGREEN
TREES

STEPPING
STONES

WOODED AREA

OPEN
LAWN AREA

DECIDUOUS CANOPY
TREES

RIVER GRAVEL
BELOW DECK

RR TIE STEPS
ANNUAL FLWS.
WOOD DECKING

VEGETABLE
GARDEN

WOOD CHIP TRAIL
TO PRIVACY DECK

SLOPE

ROCK WALL

NATIVE GRASS

NORTH
1/8" = 1'—0"

GALDIN
A
ASSOCIATES

CONCEPTUAL
LANDSCAPE DEVELOPMENT
PLAN FOR:

KAPLAN RESIDENCE
ELKHORN   NEBRASKA

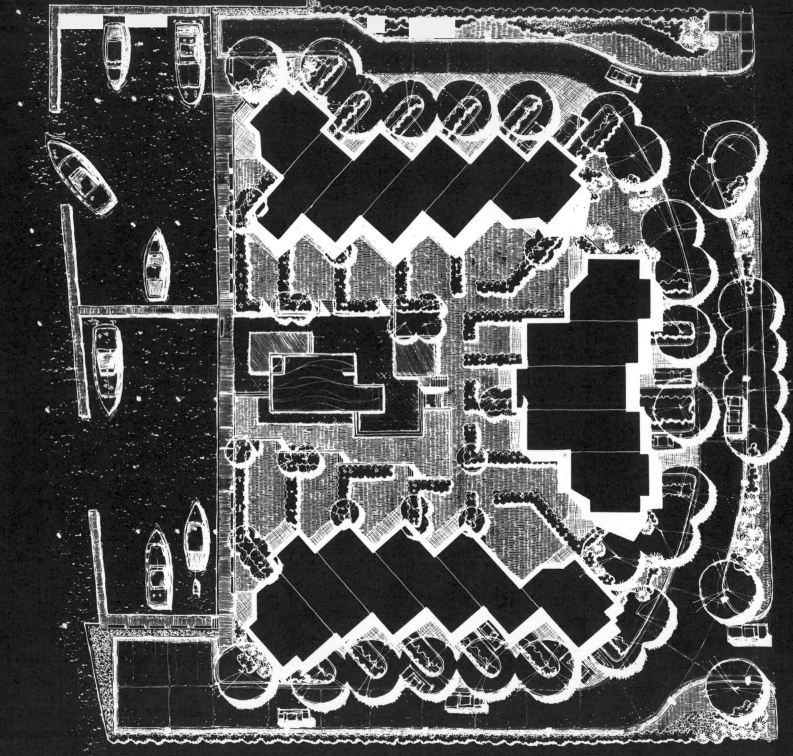

SHREWSBURY RIVER

OCEAN AVENUE · ROUTE 36

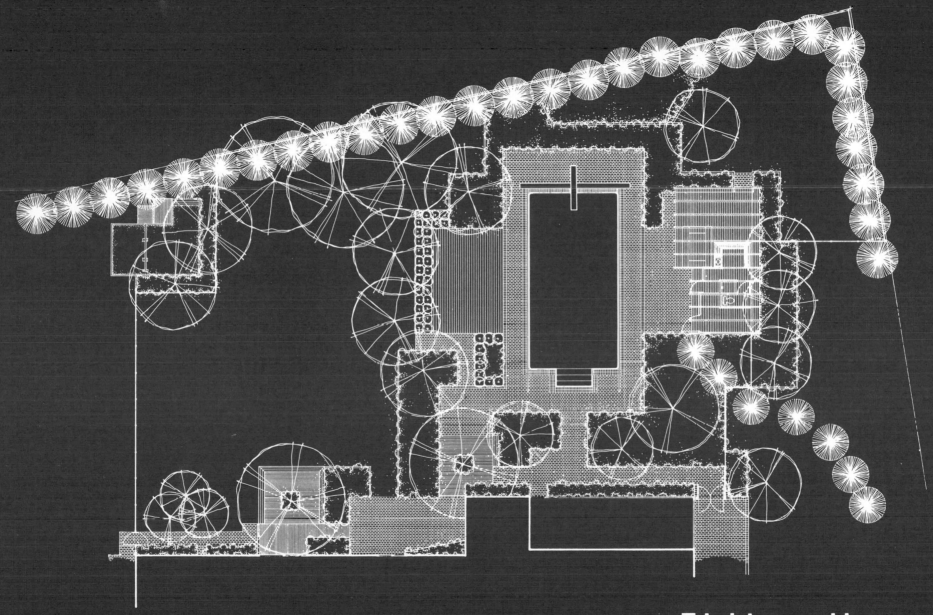

Edmiston residence
1550 Willow Lane

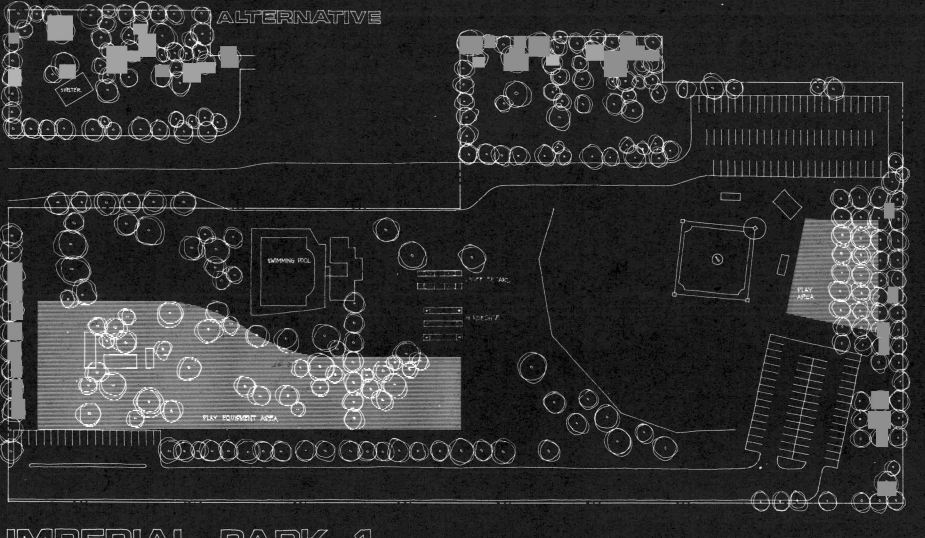

ALTERNATIVE

SHELTER

SWIMMING POOL

HUFFER CARS

HORSESHOE

PLAY AREA

PLAY EQUIPMENT AREA

IMPERIAL PARK 1

COMMUNITY RESOURCE AND RESEARCH CENTER-UNL
KIP HULVERSHORN
JANET LUTON
DON BLAIR

SCALE :   0   40'

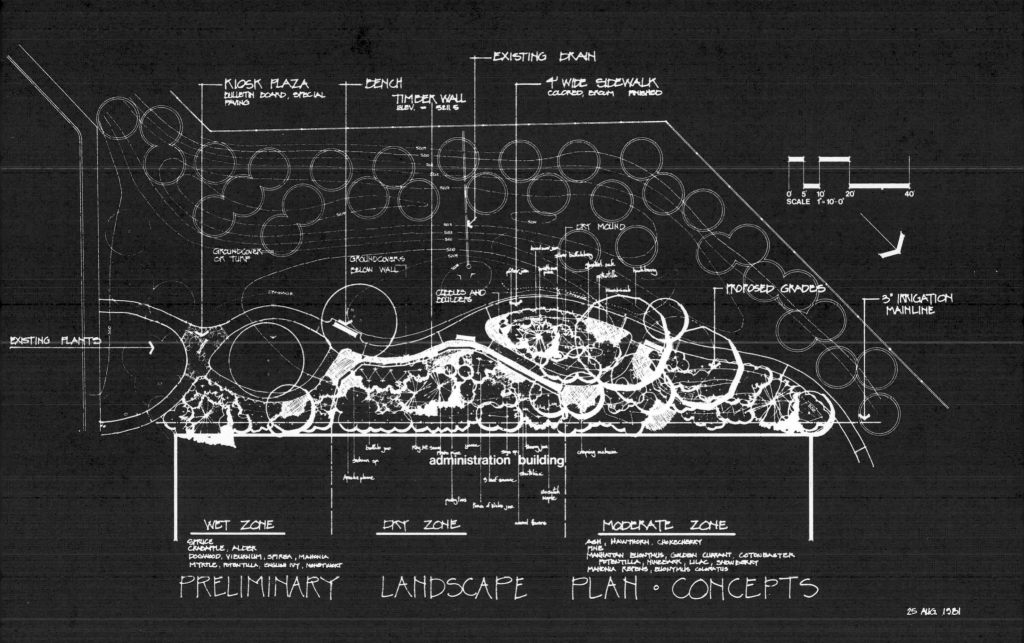

EXISTING DRAIN

KIOSK PLAZA — BENCH — 4' WIDE SIDEWALK
BULLETIN BOARD, SPECIAL PAVING   COLORED, BROOM FINISHED

TIMBER WALL
ELEV. = 5211.5

SCALE 1"=10'-0"
0 5' 10'   20'   40'

DRY MOUND

GROUNDCOVER OR TURF

GROUNDCOVERS BELOW WALL

PROPOSED GRADES

3" IRRIGATION MAINLINE

EXISTING PLANTS

COBBLES AND BOULDERS

administration building

WET ZONE

SPRUCE
CRABAPPLE, ALDER
DOGWOOD, VIBURNUM, SPIREA, MAHONIA
MYRTLE, POTENTILLA, ENGLISH IVY, MONEYWORT

DRY ZONE

MODERATE ZONE

ASH, HAWTHORN, CHOKECHERRY
PINE
MANHATTAN EUONYMUS, GOLDEN CURRANT, COTONEASTER
POTENTILLA, NINEBARK, LILAC, SNOWBERRY
MAHONIA REPENS, EUONYMUS COLORATUS

PRELIMINARY LANDSCAPE PLAN • CONCEPTS

25 AUG. 1981

OPEN SPACE
HIERARCHY
1 COMMUNITY SPACE
2 NEIGHBORHOOD SPACE
3 CLUSTER SPACE
4 INDIVIDUAL SPACE

NEIGHBORHOOD OPEN SPACE

NEIGHBORHOOD OPEN SPACE

NEIGHBORHOOD OPEN SPACE

COMMUNITY OPEN SPACE

MED/HIGH DENSITY DEVELOPMENT

3.

0 25 50   100   200

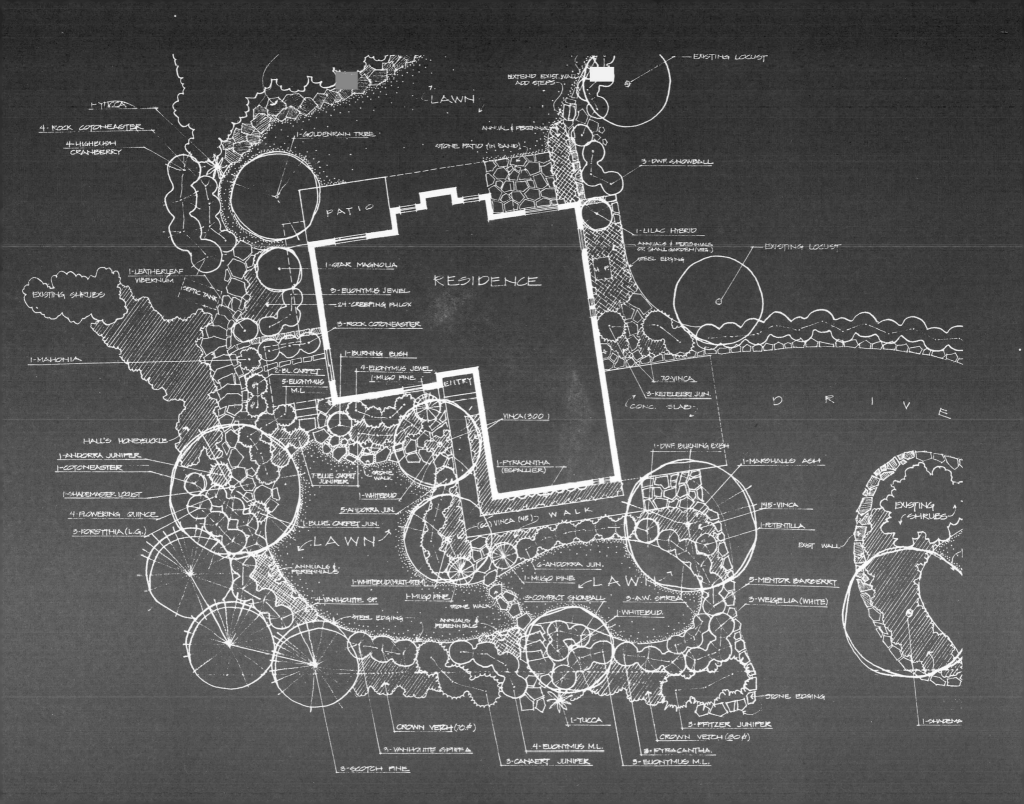

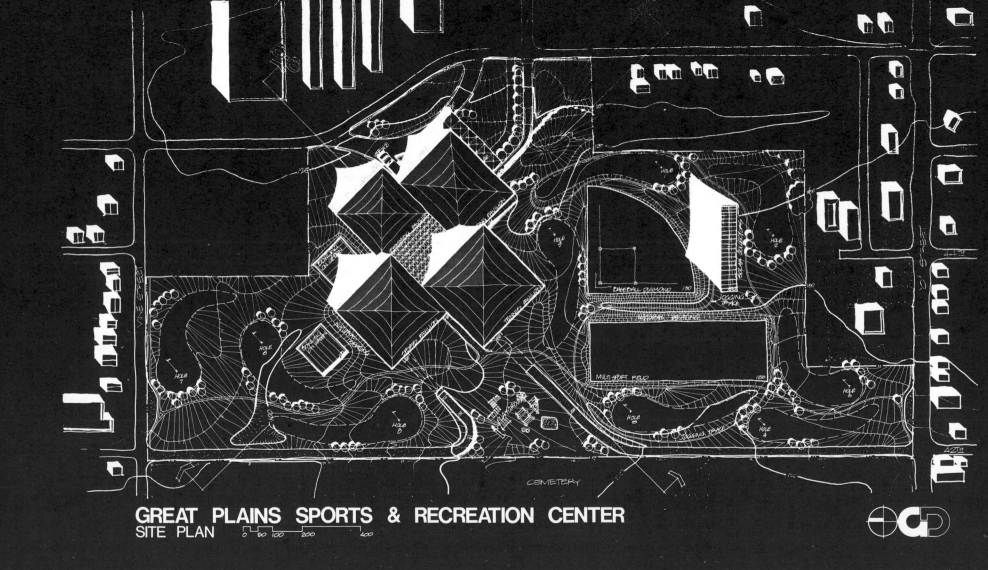

GREAT PLAINS SPORTS & RECREATION CENTER
SITE PLAN

0 50 100   200   400

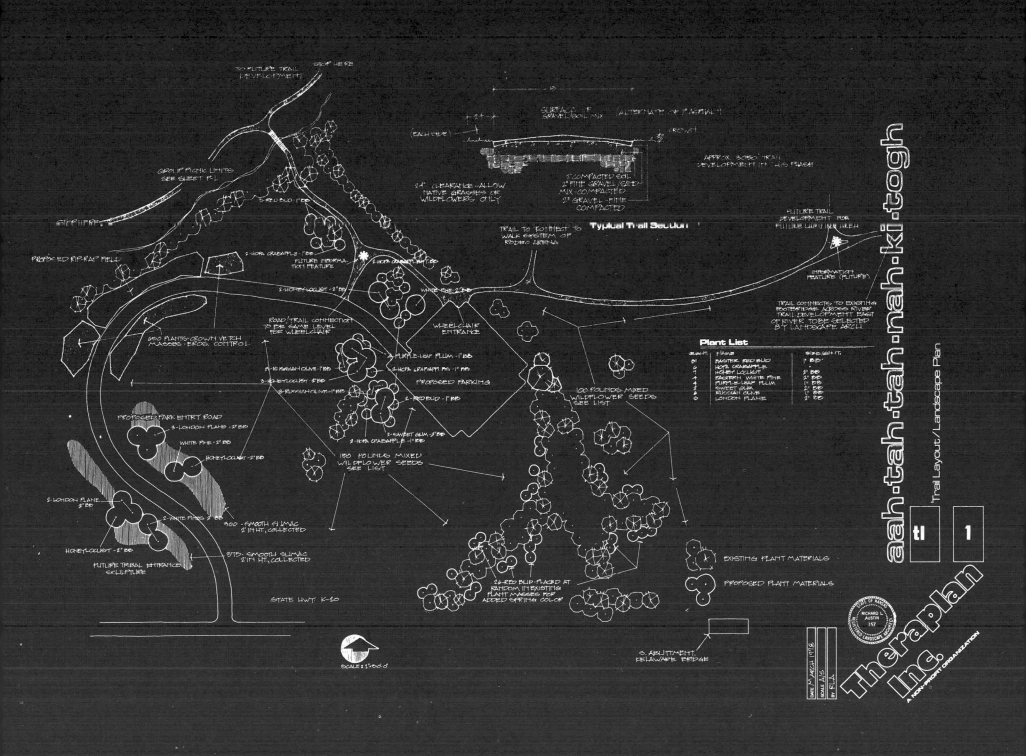

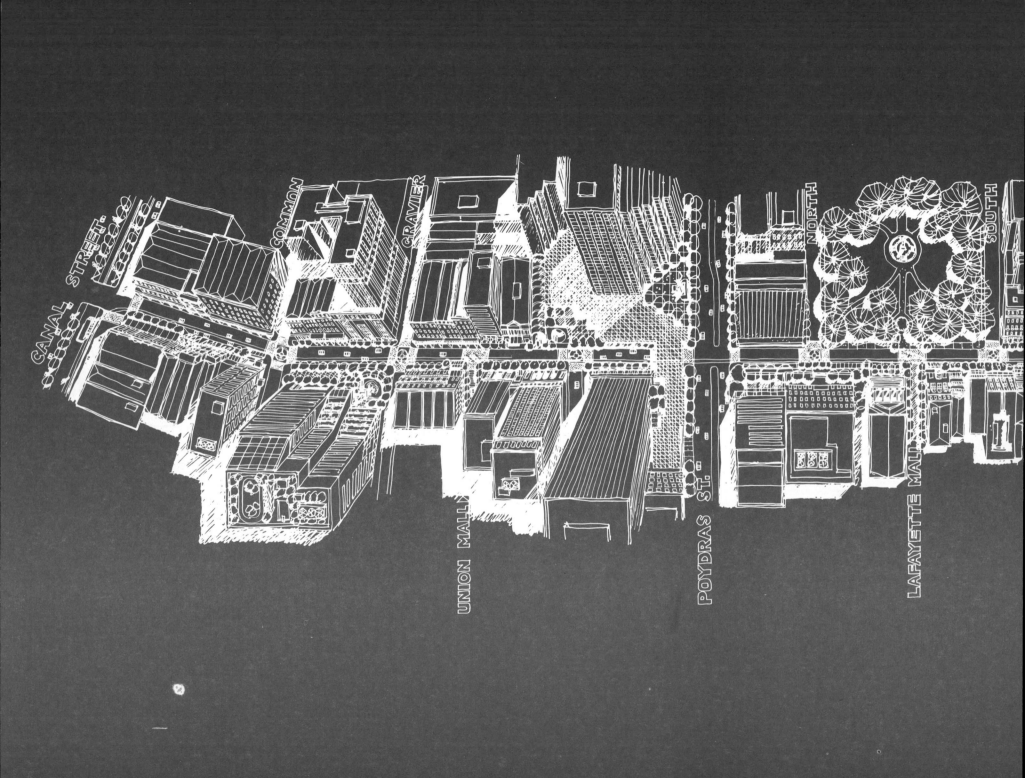

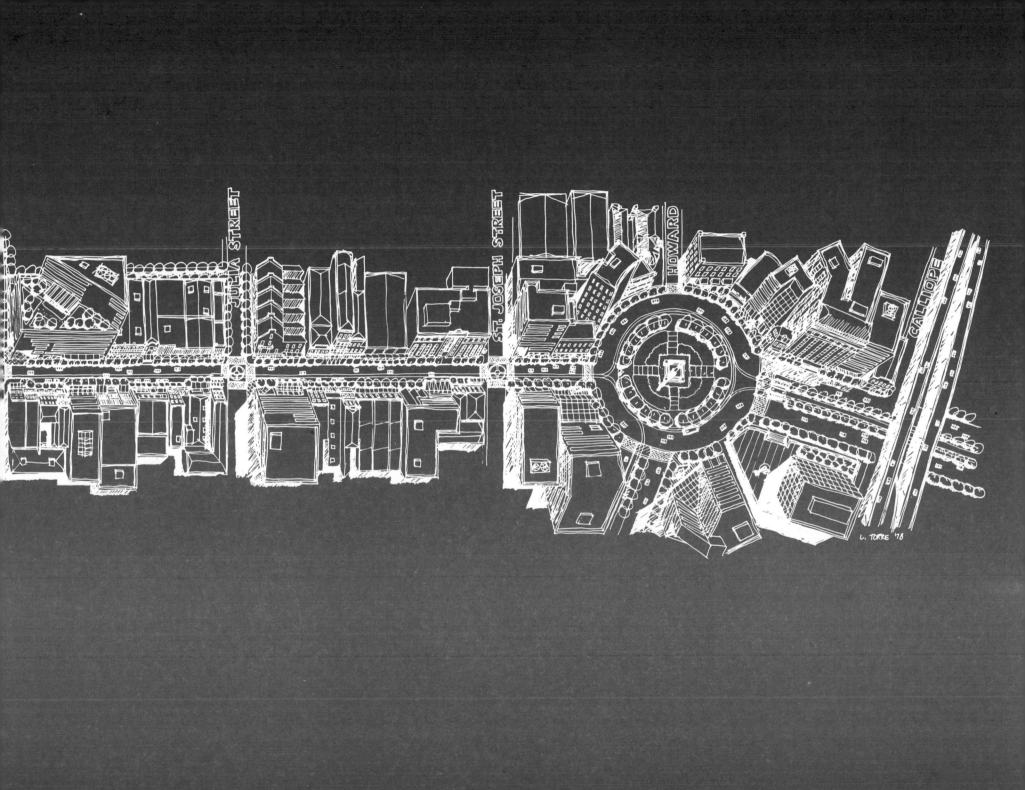

ST. JULIA STREET ST. JOSEPH STREET HOWARD CALLIOPE

L. TORRE '78

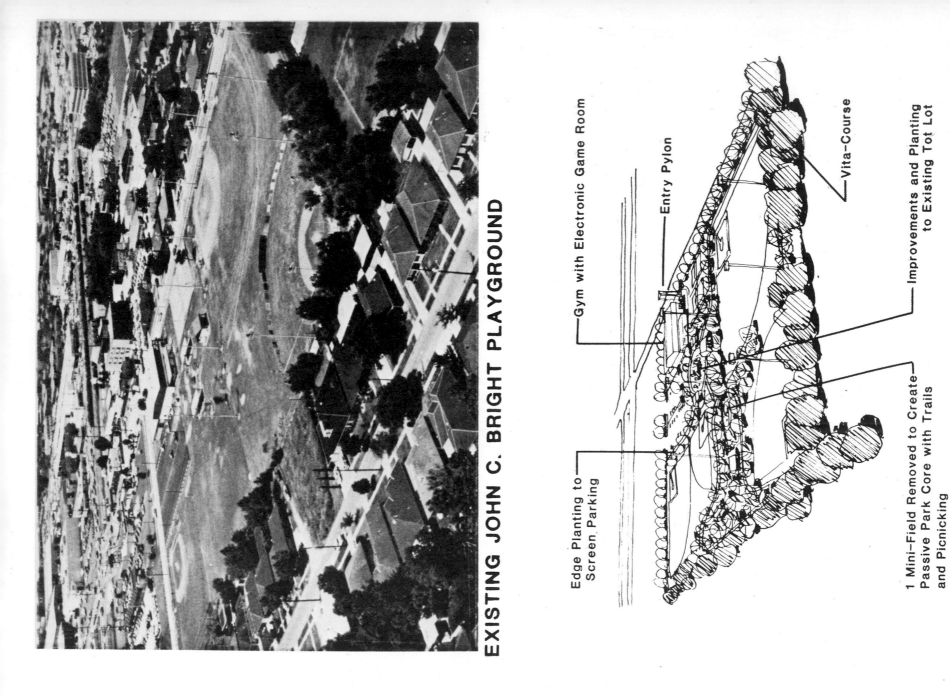

EXISTING JOHN C. BRIGHT PLAYGROUND

Gym with Electronic Game Room

Entry Pylon

Vita-Course

Improvements and Planting to Existing Tot Lot

Edge Planting to Screen Parking

1 Mini-Field Removed to Create Passive Park Core with Trails and Picnicking

PROPOSED JOHN C. BRIGHT IMPROVEMENTS

THIS TECHNIQUE EMPLOYS A PHOTOGRAPH OF THE EXISTING SITE IN ASSOCIATION WITH THE PROPOSED SKETCH OF THE DEVELOPMENT.

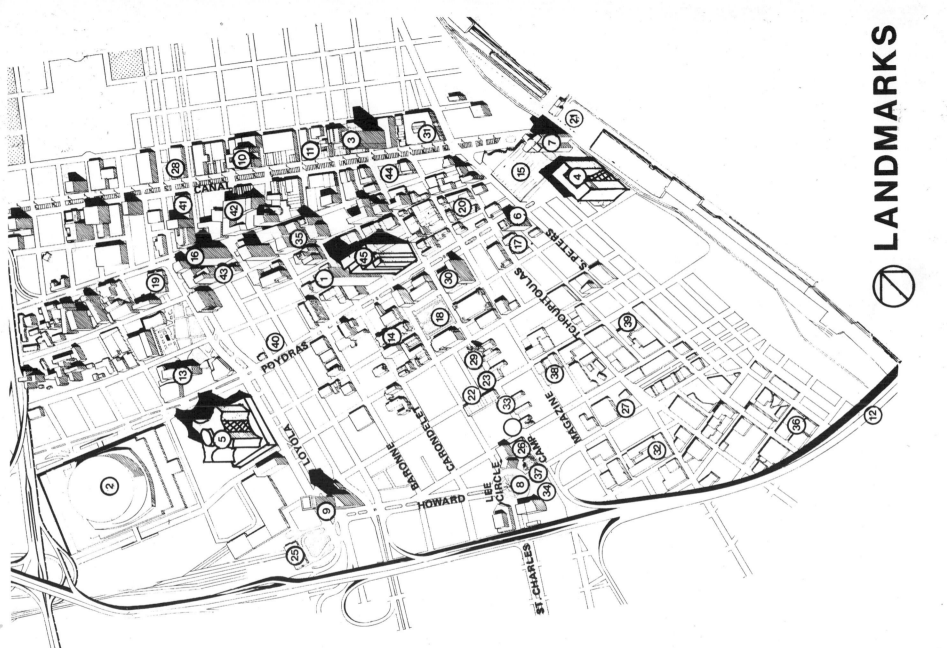

EXISTING AND PROPOSED BUILDINGS CAN
BE SKETCHED ONTO STREET PLANS FOR
ADDITIONAL SITE DEVELOPMENT EMPHASIS.

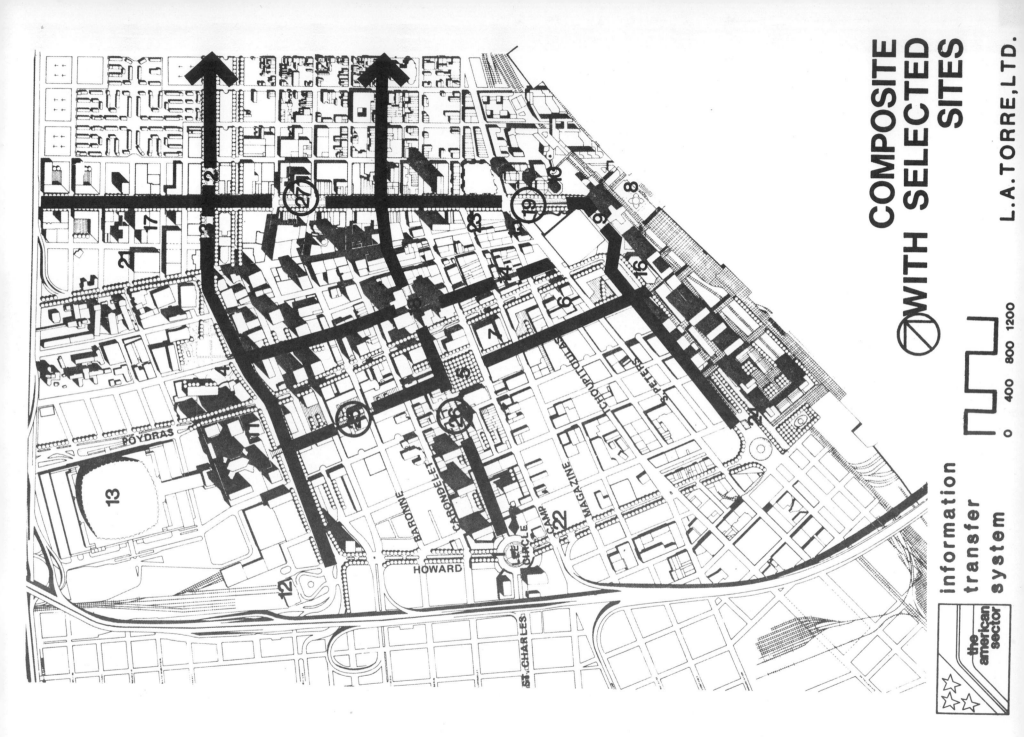

COMPOSITE
WITH SELECTED
SITES

L.A.TORRE, LTD.

information
transfer
system

the
american
sector

0   400   800 1200

POYDRAS

HOWARD

BARONNE

CARONDELET

CAMP

MAGAZINE

TCHOUPITOULAS

ST. CHARLES

13

124

PROPOSED SITE REFINEMENTS CAN BE SKETCHED ONTO PHOTOGRAPHS OF EXISTING FEATURES.

CONTRIBUTORS

The Community Resource and Research Center
University of Nebraska - Lincoln, Nebraska
   Pgs. - 22, 25, 28, 31, 32, 40, 48, 49, 54, 108, 109, 110, 114

R.E. Cunningham
Ambrose Jackson Associates
Omaha, Nebraska
   Pgs. - 16, 17, 20, 21, 26, 27, 41, 45, 85, 86, 93, 102, 106,
      107, 116, 118

The DeBord-Dunbar Partnership
Des Moines, Iowa
   Pgs. - 39, 42, 43, 55, 95, 96

The Design Consortium
New Orleans, Louisiana
   Pgs. - 1, 46, 73-83, 87, 88, 90-92, 120-125

Mr. Larry Enersen
The Clark-Enersen Partners
Lincoln, Nebraska
   Pgs. - 4, 34, 35, 72

Galpin-Giaccio Associates
Omaha, Nebraska
   Pgs. - 30, 99, 103, 104, 111

Donald H. Godi and Associates
Lakewood, Colorado
   Pgs. - 29, 98, 115

Professor Marge Koepke
Department of Landscape Architecture
Kansas State University
   Pgs. - 50, 117

McDonald Douglas Automation Company
(MCAUTO)
St. Louis, Missouri
   Pgs. - 69, 70

Professor M. Brito Mutunhayagam
University of Nebraska
   Pgs. - 62-64, 66-68

Professor William F. Scerbo
Rutgers University
New Brunswick, New Jersey
        pgs. - 44, 112

Site Planning Associates
Wichita, Kansas
        pgs. - 24, 53, 59, 97, 113

Texas Parks and Wildlife Department
Master Planing Branch
Austin, Texas
        pgs. - 8-15, 18, 19

ABOUT THE AUTHOR

RICHARD L. AUSTIN IS AN ASSOCIATE PROFESSOR IN THE COLLEGE OF ARCHITECTURE AND THE DEPARTMENT OF HORTICULTURE AT THE UNIVERSITY OF NEBRASKA-LINCOLN. HE IS THE AUTHOR OF DESIGNING WITH PLANTS, DESIGNING THE NATURAL LANDSCAPE, AND REPORT GRAPHICS PUBLISHED BY VAN NOSTRAND REINHOLD COMPANY. HE ALSO SERVES AS THE COORDINATING EDITOR OF THE YEARBOOK OF LANDSCAPE ARCHITECTURE.